LAWS AND LEGISLATION

RIGHT TO WORK LAWS AND FEDERAL LABOR RELATIONS STATUTES

AN OVERVIEW

LAWS AND LEGISLATION

Additional books in this series can be found on Nova's website under the Series tab.

Additional e-books in this series can be found on Nova's website under the e-book tab.

LAWS AND LEGISLATION

RIGHT TO WORK LAWS AND FEDERAL LABOR RELATIONS STATUTES

AN OVERVIEW

MORGAN N. BRODERICK
EDITOR

NOVINKA
New York

For permission to use material from this book please contact us:
Telephone 631-231-7269; Fax 631-231-8175
Web Site: http://www.novapublishers.com

Library of Congress Cataloging-in-Publication Data

ISBN: 978-1-62417-918-1

Published by Nova Science Publishers, Inc. † New York

CONTENTS

PREFACE

The National Labor Relations Act (NLRA) establishes most private-sector workers' rights to unionize and collectively bargain over wages, benefits, and working conditions. Enacted in 1935, the NLRA also permits collective bargaining contracts between employers and labor organizations that require every individual covered by the collective bargaining contract to pay dues to the negotiating labor organization. These contract provisions are known as union security agreements. Since the NLRA was amended by the Taft-Hartley Act in 1947, individual states have been permitted to supersede the union security provisions of the NLRA by enacting laws that prohibit union security agreements. These state laws are known as right to work (RTW) laws. This book provides a brief legislative history on RTW laws and on the federal role in the regulation of unions; a summary of the origin and developments of RTW laws, recent events at the state level, and federal labor relations statutes.

Chapter 1 - The National Labor Relations Act (NLRA) establishes most private-sector workers' rights to unionize and collectively bargain over wages, benefits, and working conditions. Enacted in 1935, the NLRA also permits collective bargaining contracts between employers and labor organizations that require every individual covered by the collective bargaining contract to pay dues to the negotiating labor organization. These contract provisions are known as union security agreements. Since the NLRA was amended by the Taft-Hartley Act in 1947, individual states have been permitted to supersede the union security provisions of the NLRA by enacting laws that prohibit union security agreements. These state laws are known as right to work (RTW) laws.

Currently, 23 states have RTW laws. Of these, 12 states passed RTW laws prior to 1950 and another six passed them prior to 1960. The two most recent states to adopt RTW laws are Oklahoma (2001) and Indiana (2012). Several other state legislatures are debating RTW laws.

Recent legislative proposals, with substantial numbers of cosponsors, would expand RTW policies nationwide. Advocates of national RTW laws claim that they would enhance personal freedom and employer flexibility. Opponents argue that such laws would weaken workers' abilities to collectively bargain for more favorable compensation and working conditions. Proposals aiming to expand RTW policies typically strike the provisions of the NLRA that permit union security agreements.

National RTW proposals are often discussed in the context of the economic performance of states that have adopted them. However, research that compares outcomes in RTW and union security states is inconclusive. The recent data trends between RTW and union security states are relatively distinct, but the influence of RTW laws in these trends (if any) is unclear.

- Unionization rates in RTW states are less than half of what they are in union security states. It is ambiguous what portion of this difference is attributable to RTW laws and what portion is due to diverse preferences among the states regarding unionization.
- In the past decade, aggregate employment in RTW states has increased modestly while employment in union security states has declined. It is unclear if this growth is attributable to RTW, other pro-business policies (which tend to be concentrated in RTW states), or other factors.
- Wages are lower in RTW states than union security states. Historical research has suggested that RTW laws have little influence on these differences. More contemporary scholarship has come to diverse conclusions, depending on the researchers' methodology.

Difficulties associated with rigorously studying the relationships between RTW laws and various outcomes are likely to continue to make it difficult to generate definitive findings about these relationships. As such, the ongoing debate on RTW may be driven by factors other than rigorous empirical evidence.

Chapter 2 - Since 1926, Congress has enacted three major laws that govern labor-management relations for private sector and federal employees. An issue for Congress is the effect of these laws on employers, workers, and the nation's economy. The Bureau of Labor Statistics estimates that, nationwide, 14.8 million employees are union members. In the 112th Congress alone, more than 30 bills were introduced to amend federal labor relations statutes. The proposals ranged from making union recognition without a secret ballot election illegal to further modifying runoff election procedures. These legislative activities, and the significant number of employees affected by federal labor relations laws, illustrate the current relevance of labor relations issues to legislators and their constituents.

The three major labor relations statutes in the United States are the Railway Labor Act, the National Labor Relations Act, and the Federal Service Labor-Management Relations Statute. Each law governs a distinct population of the U.S. workforce.

The Railway Labor Act (RLA) was enacted in 1926, and its coverage extends to railway and airline carriers, unions, and employees of the carriers. The RLA guarantees employees the right to organize and collectively bargain with their employers over conditions of work and protects them against unfair employer and union practices. It lays out specific procedures for selecting employee representatives and provides a dispute resolution system that aims to efficiently resolve labor disputes between parties, with an emphasis on mediation and arbitration. The RLA provides multiple processes for dispute resolution, depending on whether the dispute is based on a collective bargaining issue or the application of an existing collective bargaining agreement.

The National Labor Relations Act (NLRA) was enacted in 1935. The NLRA's coverage extends to most other private sector businesses that are not covered by the RLA. Like the RLA, the NLRA guarantees employees the right to organize and collectively bargain over conditions of employment and protects them against unfair employer and union activities. However, its dispute resolution system differs from the RLA's in that it is arguably more adversarial in nature; many disputes are resolved through adjudication, rather than through mediation and arbitration.

The Federal Service Labor-Management Relations Statute (FSLMRS) was enacted in 1978, and its coverage extends to most federal employees. The basic framework of the FSLMRS is similar to that of the NLRA; however, employee rights are more restricted under the FSLMRS, given the unique nature of their employer, the federal government. Federal employees have the right to organize and collectively bargain, but they cannot bargain over wages or strike. Additionally, the President has the power to unilaterally exclude an agency or subdivision from coverage under the FSLMRS if he determines that its primary work concerns national security.

This report provides a brief history and overview of the aims of each of these statutes. It also discusses key statutory provisions for each statute.

Congress has enacted three major laws that govern labor-management relations. The first law, the Railway Labor Act (RLA), was enacted in 1926. The RLA applies to railway and airline carriers. In 1935, Congress passed the National Labor Relations Act (NLRA), which applies to private sector employers other than railroad and airline carriers, and in 1978, Congress enacted the Federal Service Labor-Management Relations Statute (FSLMRS), which applies to most federal employees. This report provides an overview of these three labor relations laws by giving a brief history of each law and discussing how each statute operates and is administered.

This report uses specific "terms of art" relevant to these acts. Appendix A defines these "terms of art." Appendix B provides a list of acronyms used in this report. Appendix C contains a table that compares provisions of all three laws.

In: Right to Work Laws …
Editor: Morgan N. Broderick

ISBN: 978-1-62417-918-1

Chapter 1

RIGHT TO WORK LAWS: LEGISLATIVE BACKGROUND AND EMPIRICAL RESEARCH*

Benjamin Collins

SUMMARY

The National Labor Relations Act (NLRA) establishes most private-sector workers' rights to unionize and collectively bargain over wages, benefits, and working conditions. Enacted in 1935, the NLRA also permits collective bargaining contracts between employers and labor organizations that require every individual covered by the collective bargaining contract to pay dues to the negotiating labor organization. These contract provisions are known as union security agreements. Since the NLRA was amended by the Taft-Hartley Act in 1947, individual states have been permitted to supersede the union security provisions of the NLRA by enacting laws that prohibit union security agreements. These state laws are known as right to work (RTW) laws.

Currently, 23 states have RTW laws. Of these, 12 states passed RTW laws prior to 1950 and another six passed them prior to 1960. The two most recent states to adopt RTW laws are Oklahoma (2001) and Indiana (2012). Several other state legislatures are debating RTW laws.

* This is an edited, reformatted and augmented version of the Congressional Research Service Publication, CRS Report for Congress R42575, dated December 6, 2012.

Recent legislative proposals, with substantial numbers of cosponsors, would expand RTW policies nationwide. Advocates of national RTW laws claim that they would enhance personal freedom and employer flexibility. Opponents argue that such laws would weaken workers' abilities to collectively bargain for more favorable compensation and working conditions. Proposals aiming to expand RTW policies typically strike the provisions of the NLRA that permit union security agreements.

National RTW proposals are often discussed in the context of the economic performance of states that have adopted them. However, research that compares outcomes in RTW and union security states is inconclusive. The recent data trends between RTW and union security states are relatively distinct, but the influence of RTW laws in these trends (if any) is unclear.

- Unionization rates in RTW states are less than half of what they are in union security states. It is ambiguous what portion of this difference is attributable to RTW laws and what portion is due to diverse preferences among the states regarding unionization.
- In the past decade, aggregate employment in RTW states has increased modestly while employment in union security states has declined. It is unclear if this growth is attributable to RTW, other pro-business policies (which tend to be concentrated in RTW states), or other factors.
- Wages are lower in RTW states than union security states. Historical research has suggested that RTW laws have little influence on these differences. More contemporary scholarship has come to diverse conclusions, depending on the researchers' methodology.

Difficulties associated with rigorously studying the relationships between RTW laws and various outcomes are likely to continue to make it difficult to generate definitive findings about these relationships. As such, the ongoing debate on RTW may be driven by factors other than rigorous empirical evidence.

BACKGROUND

To promote commerce and deter labor unrest, Congress has established laws regulating unionization and collective bargaining (i.e., similar workers negotiating compensation and working conditions as a unit rather than individually). The primary federal legislation that regulates private sector collective bargaining is the National Labor Relations Act (NLRA), enacted in 1935. In addition to establishing workers' rights to organize and establishing union election procedures, the NLRA also permits collective bargaining contracts between employers and labor organizations that require all workers covered by the contract to pay dues to the negotiating organization. These contract provisions are known as *union security agreements*.[1]

Since the NLRA was amended by the Taft-Hartley Act in 1947, individual states have had the option of enacting laws that prohibit union security agreements. These state laws supersede the union security provisions of the NLRA and are known as *right to work* (RTW) laws. As of this writing, 23 states have enacted RTW laws.

Since the Taft-Hartley Act, changes to federal law relating to unionization and RTW have been limited. Debate on this topic, however, has been ongoing and there have been legislative proposals to both expand and prohibit RTW laws. Supporters of expanding RTW laws claim that they will increase personal freedom and employer flexibility. Conversely, supporters of proposals to eliminate RTW laws emphasize that unions must negotiate on behalf of all workers in the unit, and as such, it is appropriate that all workers pay for that for representation.

This report is divided into two parts. The first part discusses RTW laws themselves. It provides a brief legislative history on the federal role in the regulation of unions, a summary of the origin and development of RTW laws, a discussion of recent events at the state level, and federal legislation related to RTW. The second part of the report reviews the varied empirical research on the effects of RTW laws. Specifically, it will discuss the mixed evidence indicating relationships between RTW laws and other economic outcomes.

LEGISLATIVE HISTORY

Prior to the passage of the federal labor laws discussed in this report, the regulation of labor and collective bargaining was left to the states. Laws varied, but most states adopted policies of open competition with minimal governmental regulations.[2]

In 1926, the Railway Labor Act was the first federal law to guarantee collective bargaining rights to a group of workers. The Norris-LaGuardia Act, passed in 1932, prohibited federal courts from issuing an injunction in any labor dispute. Previously, judges could end a strike if they did not approve of its methods or objectives. The Norris-LaGuardia Act, however, did not guarantee collective bargaining rights; it merely regulated employer-union relations once they were established.

National Labor Relations Act[3]

Enacted in 1935, the NLRA governs labor-management relations and collective bargaining for most private sector workers.[4] The NLRA is also known as the Wagner Act. Many provisions of the NLRA were contained in the National Industrial Recovery Act (NIRA), which was enacted in 1933 but found unconstitutional in 1935. The Supreme Court upheld the NLRA in 1937.

The NLRA found that the refusals of employers to collectively bargain with employees "lead to strikes and other forms of industrial strife or unrest, which have the intent or the necessary effect of burdening or obstructing commerce[.]"[5] To remedy this issue, the NLRA guarantees workers the right to organize and bargain collectively over wages, hours, and conditions of employment. It also establishes procedures for the election and certification of unions and establishes certain unfair labor practices for employers that may discourage workers from unionizing. The NLRA is enforced by the National Labor Relations Board (NLRB), an independent federal agency.

The NLRA also permits collective bargaining contracts to contain union security agreements that require all workers covered under the contract to pay dues to the negotiating labor organization.

Taft-Hartley Act

Passed over a presidential veto in 1947, the Taft-Hartley Act (also known as the Labor Management Relations Act) substantially amended the NLRA. Many of the provisions in the Taft-Hartley Act, including the statement of purpose at the beginning, remain in current law.

Whereas the original Wagner Act focused on asserting the rights of workers and organized labor, the Taft-Hartley Act addresses employers, employees, and labor unions as equal parties in the negotiation process and states that "neither party has any right in its relations with any other to engage in acts or practices which jeopardize the public health, safety, or interest." It supplemented existing unfair labor practices for employers by establishing unfair labor practices for unions. It also prohibited secondary strikes and outlawed so-called "closed shops" that required an employee to be a union member prior to being hired.

The Taft-Hartley amendments also established the RTW provisions that are still part of the NLRA. These provisions stated that individual states may pass laws prohibiting union security agreements in labor contracts and that these state laws would supersede the NLRA provisions authorizing union security agreements.[6]

Legislation Since Taft-Hartley

Amendments to the NLRA since 1947 have been limited. In 1959, the Landrum-Griffin Act increased regulation of internal union activities and enumerated certain rights to all union members.[7] Subsequent legislation in 1974 expanded the provisions of the NLRA to employees of private nonprofit hospitals, a population that had been excluded from coverage since the enactment of the Taft-Hartley Act.

In 1980, the NLRA was amended to permit individuals who were covered by a union security agreement but were members of a religion that objected to financially supporting a labor union to pay the equivalent of the union dues to a charitable organization.[8] No major federal legislation related to the NLRA or RTW has been enacted since 1980, though there has been ongoing debate on the issue.

UNION SECURITY AGREEMENTS AND REQUIRED UNION DUES

In states without RTW laws, an elected union and an employer can agree to a collective bargaining contract that requires all workers covered by the contract to become members within 30 days.[9] Workplaces covered by such an agreement are often called *union shops*.

In 1963, the Supreme Court ruled that, even in a union shop, an employee cannot be required to join a union pursuant to a union security agreement. Instead, the employee may pay dues but decline to become a full union member.[10] Dues-paying nonmembers are referred to as *financial core members*. In spite of their name, financial core members are not union members: they may not participate in union activities or even vote on the ratification of the collective bargaining contract that covers them. Financial core members are not subject to union bylaws or union discipline but they are subject to the rights and responsibilities in the collective bargaining contract with their employer.

Subsequent decisions have concluded that financial core members only need to pay dues to cover the cost of collective bargaining functions. These functions include bargaining, contract administration, and grievance adjustment. Financial core members do not have to financially support union functions that are unrelated to collective bargaining such as political activities. Workers subject to a union security agreement must be informed of the financial core membership option.[11]

An alternative to the union shop is the *agency shop*. In an agency shop, workers covered by a collective bargaining contract are required to pay a fee for representation (an *agency fee*) but are not required to join the union. Since union shop agreements must permit covered workers to forego union membership and only pay a representation fee, union shops and agency shops operate similarly in practice.

In cases where a union security agreement conflicts with a worker's religious beliefs, the objecting worker may donate the equivalent of the agency fee or financial core dues to a non- labor, non-religious charity.[12]

Union Security and Workers Not Covered by the NLRA

The collective bargaining rights of several groups of workers are covered by legislation other than the NLRA. Union security agreements among these groups are governed by other federal laws:

- Interstate railway and airline employees' collective bargaining rights are defined by the Railway Labor Act (RLA).[13] The RLA permits union security agreements in all states, effectively superseding any local RTW laws.[14]
- Postal workers' collective bargaining rights are defined by the Postal Reorganization Act of 1970. The act specifies that dues will be deducted from an employee's pay only with the written authorization of that employee.[15] This optional deduction applies in all states.
- Federal employees' collective bargaining rights are defined in the Federal Service Labor-Management Relations Statute (FSLMRS).[16] It specifies that dues will only be deducted from an employee's pay upon written authorization from that employee.[17] The FSLMRS applies equally in both RTW and union security states.

State Right to Work Laws

The Taft-Hartley amendments to the NLRA permit individual states to pass laws that prohibit union security agreements. Table 1 lists the 23 states that have passed such laws. A state may pursue RTW through legislation, a ballot initiative, or an amendment to its state constitution.

The details of RTW laws vary by state. The law passed by Indiana in February 2012, for example, excluded employees of the state, employees of "a political subdivision," and several other groups that are not covered by the NLRA.[18] Conversely, the constitutional amendment passed in Oklahoma is broader and includes all workers in the state.

The breadth of some state laws that have attempted to regulate workers who are not covered by the NLRA has been challenged in the courts. For example, both a federal appeals court and the Oklahoma supreme court have determined that Oklahoma's prohibition of union security agreements does not extend to workers covered by the Railway Labor Act.[19]

RECENT DEVELOPMENTS

Federal Legislation

While changes to federal law regarding unions and RTW have been limited in recent decades, debate has been robust and ongoing. Congress has considered a number of proposals that would amend the NLRA's provisions regarding union security agreements. These proposals have ranged from striking the provisions that permit union security agreements (effectively making every state an RTW state) to striking the provisions that allow individuals states to prohibit union security agreements (effectively invalidating existing RTW laws).

Since the 104th Congress, a National Right to Work bill has been introduced in the House during the first session of each Congress. Similar bills have regularly been introduced in the Senate during this time. These bills would amend the NLRA by striking the language that permits union security agreements and would make similar changes to the Railway Labor Act. Most national RTW proposals are relatively narrow in scope and only prohibit union security agreements. They typically do not address union election procedures or any other issues associated with collective bargaining. These National Right to Work proposals often have a substantial number of cosponsors.[20]

Contrasting proposals that would strike the provisions of the NLRA that allow states to enact RTW laws have also been introduced in recent Congresses. These proposals have been introduced with much less regularity than National Right to Work proposals. These proposals typically forbid state RTW laws by striking the provisions of the NLRA that permit such laws.[21]

State Activities

As noted previously, Indiana is the most recent state to enact an RTW law. Since Indiana's enactment of its RTW law, several state legislatures, including those in Ohio, Michigan, and New Hampshire have debated RTW laws, but none have enacted one.

Empirical Evidence Relating to RTW

There has been a great deal of debate and research on the effects of RTW laws on states that adopt them. Most empirical research has concluded that RTW laws have a negative relationship with unionization rates (also known as union density) though the causal effect is debated. The effects of RTW laws on other economic outcomes, such as job growth and wages, have been studied, though findings have been mixed and there is no broad consensus on the magnitude (if any) of the effects of these laws.

Limitations on Measuring the Effects of RTW Laws

It is important to recognize that *there is no straightforward way to measure how RTW laws affect other outcomes*. It is possible to compare data from states with RTW laws to states without such laws, but since it is not possible to observe the counterfactual—what would have happened in each state if it had a differing union security policy—there is no simple way to tell what contribution an RTW law (or lack thereof) made to other outcomes in the state. For example, a researcher could compare employment growth in Arizona (an RTW state) and neighboring New Mexico (a union security state), but it would be impossible to identify what portion of the differences between the states was attributable to their respective union security laws and what portions were attributable to differences in labor force characteristics, industry makeup, local taxation policies, and countless other state-specific characteristics. While it is not possible to completely isolate the effect of RTW laws in dynamic and complex economies, some researchers have attempted to estimate the effect of RTW laws by controlling for other factors. Their techniques have varied and it comes as little surprise that diverse methodologies have yielded diverse conclusions. The subsequent review of RTW-related studies does not attempt to be exhaustive. It does, however, attempt to cover frequently cited studies as well as more recent studies that attempt to isolate the effect of RTW laws on various outcomes.

Table 1. Right to Work States and Date of Enactment

State	Year of Enactment	State	Year of Enactment
Florida	1943[a]	Nevada	1951
Arizona	1947	Alabama	1953
Arkansas	1947	Mississippi	1954
Georgia	1947	South Carolina	1954
Iowa	1947	Utah	1955
Nebraska	1947	Kansas	1958
North Carolina	1947	Wyoming	1963
North Dakota	1947	Louisiana	1976
South Dakota	1947	Idaho	1985
Tennessee	1947	Oklahoma	2001
Texas	1947[b]	Indiana	2012
Virginia	1947		

Source: U.S. Department of Labor, Wage and Hour Division, http://www.dol.gov/whd/state

Note: Sources vary on date of enactment. The table reflects the source cited above as well as the recent enactment of RTW in Indiana.

a. While it was originally enacted in 1943, the validity of Florida's RTW law was unclear until the enactment of the Taft-Hartley Act.

b. Texas originally passed RTW in 1947, though the law was modified to its current form in 1993.

Right to Work and Unionization

Table 2 shows the rate of union membership and the share of workers represented by a union in RTW and union security states. Two intuitive trends emerge. First, the union membership rate in union security states is nearly three times that of RTW states (15.8% vs. 5.7%). Second, the proportion of workers who are covered by a union contract but who are not members of the union is higher in RTW states than union security states. In RTW states, about 18% of the workers who are covered by a union contract are non-members (approximately 616,000 of 3.4 million). In union security states, this share is about 7% (about 910,000 of 12.8 million).

Table 2. Union Membership and Representation by Sector and in Right to Work and Union Security States, 2011

	Employment (in thousands)	Union Members (in thousands)	% Union Members	Covered by Union Contract (in thousands)	% Covered by Union Contract
Total	**125,210**	**14,755**	**11.8%**	**16,281**	**13.0%**
RTW	49,604	2,812	5.7%	3,428	6.9%
Union Security	75,606	11,943	15.8%	12,853	17.0%
Private Sector					
Total	104,778	7,204	6.9%	7,972	7.6%
RTW	41,182	1,350	3.3%	1,602	3.9%
Union Security	63,596	5,855	9.2%	6,370	10.0%
Public Sector					
Total	20,432	7,550	37.0%	8,309	40.7%
RTW	8,421	1,462	17.4%	1,827	21.7%
Union Security	12,010	6,088	50.7%	6,482	54.0%

Source: Current Population Survey. State-level data were disaggregated by sector by Barry Hirsch and David Macpherson and posted at http://www.unionstats.com/. In this presentation, CRS has divided the data into RTW and union security states.

Note: Data are limited to wage and salary workers. Due to rounding, the sum of subgroups may not equal the corresponding larger groups. Due to varied data sources, employment levels may not be comparable to other tables. In accordance with its status in 2011, Indiana was classified as a union security state.

Researchers have posited many hypotheses to explain the divergent unionization rates between RTW and union security states and three common hypotheses are discussed below. These hypotheses are not mutually exclusive and can exert a collective effect on local unionization levels.[22]

The *tastes hypothesis* suggests that RTW laws reflect a state's preexisting opposition to unions and that the diversity in RTW laws simply reflects diversity in preferences toward unions. Under this hypothesis, RTW laws have no independent effect on labor organizing: RTW states have lower rates of unionization because that is the preference of workers in those states.

Examination of state-level unionization data shows support for the hypothesis that there was below-average union density in states before they passed RTW laws. Among the four states to pass RTW laws in the past 40 years, all of them had unionization rates below the national average prior to passage. Indiana was close to the national average (11.3% statewide vs. 11.8% nationally in 2011) but the three remaining states—Oklahoma (6.9% vs. 13.0% in 2000), Idaho (12.2% vs. 18.2% in 1985), and Louisiana (16.9% vs. 24.6% in 1975)—were substantially lower. The case of Idaho is particularly unique, as the unionization rate in that state fell from 23.1% in 1981 to 12.2% in 1985. In this case, a drop in unionization preceded the passage of an RTW law, a sequence that is consistent with the tastes hypothesis but not with either of the other hypotheses discussed below.

The *free-rider hypothesis* suggests that by making dues payment optional, RTW laws lead to workers covered by a collective bargaining contract declining to pay dues. This leads to a decreased number of dues-paying members having to pay more for representation. The higher dues may exceed remaining members' willingness to pay for representation and more workers may stop paying dues, eventually leading to unsustainably high dues for the remaining members. Alternately, remaining workers may decline to pay higher dues, but this may restrict the representation services available to them.

As noted above, the share of covered nonpaying workers relative to total workers covered by a union contract is higher in RTW states than union security states. A 1995 study by Sobel divided covered nonpaying workers into "true free riders" (those who valued union representation and would join the union if dues were compulsory) and "induced free riders" (those who did not value representation and would seek other employment if dues were compulsory). The study estimated that, in RTW states, about 70% of free riders were induced free riders. This means that only 30% of covered nonmembers in RTW states were free riding in the traditional sense.[23]

The *bargaining power hypothesis* is related to the free rider hypothesis and suggests that RTW laws reduce the bargaining power of unions and lead to reduced membership in the long run. Under this hypothesis, unions have less incentive to organize since they know only a portion of the workers covered by the collective bargaining contract will pay dues. This reduces organization and, in the long run, the prevalence of union jobs.

Empirical support for this hypothesis comes from a 1987 study by Ellwood and Fine, which looked at changes in new union organizing efforts after the passage of RTW laws. The study found that in the five years after states passed an RTW law, union organization fell 28% and union organizing success fell 46%. The same study found that these effects faded in subsequent years but that they may lead to a permanent decline in unionization levels.[24]

The evidence from each of these intersecting hypotheses underscores the complexity of isolating the effect of RTW laws' actual effect on unionization.

Long-Term Trends in Unionization

While there is debate as to the magnitude of influence RTW laws exert on unionization levels, there is little debate that there has been a long-term decline in unionization that is independent of RTW policies. As **Table 3** shows, union density has declined in both RTW and union security states since 1983. The share of workers covered by a collective bargaining contract (i.e., union members plus covered workers who are not members) has followed a similar trend.

Table 3. Union Membership Rates in Right to Work and Union Security States, 1983-2011

	1983	1991	2001	2011
Total	20.1%	16.1%	13.5%	11.8%
RTW	11.6%[a]	8.5%[b]	6.8%[c]	5.7%
Union Security	24.3%	20.2%	17.5%	15.8%

Source: Current Population Survey. State-level data were developed by Barry Hirsch and David Macpherson and posted at http://www.unionstats.com/. In this presentation, CRS has divided the data into RTW and union security states.

Note: 1983 is the first year for which state-level data are available. Data are limited to wage and salary workers.

a. Includes the 20 states that had passed RTW laws by 1983.

b. Includes the 20 states that had passed RTW laws by 1983 and Idaho.

c. Includes the 20 states that had passed RTW laws by 1983, Idaho, and Oklahoma.

This nationwide decline in union density further complicates analysis of RTW laws. For example, an RTW state's decline in unionization could be attributable to the RTW law, other state-level factors, or it could be influenced by a broader decline in unionization across the country.

Right to Work and Economic Outcomes

Given the complexity of establishing the relationship between RTW and first-order outcomes like unionization rates, it comes as little surprise that the literature related to the laws' effects on higher-order outcomes such as employment and wages is inconclusive. Studies have yielded a variety of conclusions, largely dependent on how researchers conduct their analyses.

The remainder of this report will summarize existing (and frequently conflicting) data and scholarship related to RTW laws. It will discuss broad statistical trends, as well as several of the more sophisticated studies available that attempt to control for other factors and isolate the effect of RTW laws.

Right to Work and Employment

Broadly speaking, there are two competing views regarding the relationship between RTW laws and employment growth:

- One view is that RTW laws create a favorable business environment in which employers have increased flexibility in hiring, discharge, and wage-setting. Businesses are attracted to this environment and employment in these areas increases.
- The competing view is that business location decisions are driven by issues such as the local labor supply and investment incentives (e.g., subsidies or tax abatements). Under this view, RTW laws are a relatively insignificant factor in the location of a business.

Table 4 presents data on employment levels for RTW and union security states between 2001 and 2011. Aggregate employment growth was clearly greater in states with RTW laws and RTW advocates often cite these trends as evidence that RTW leads to increased job growth and employment levels.[25]

Opponents of RTW laws, however, argue that aggregate data are misleading and mask substantial variation among both RTW and union security states. For example, during the 2001-2011 period illustrated in Table 4, employment grew 13.7% and 8.9%, respectively, in the union security states of Alaska and Montana while declining 3.5% and 2.2%, respectively, in the RTW states of Mississippi and Alabama. Skeptics of RTW laws' effect on employment suggest that these diverse outcomes show that RTW laws themselves do not lead to above-average employment growth.[26]

Skeptics of the relationship between RTW laws and increased employment also note that RTW laws often exist alongside other, perhaps more compelling, pro-business policies. For example, North Dakota reported the nation's fastest employment growth between 2001 and 2011. While it is an RTW state, North Dakota also sponsors a multitude of other business-oriented policies such as tax exemptions, subsidized training, and other financial incentives.[27] North Dakota's growth may also have been attributable to non-policy characteristics such as an above-average presence of natural resources.

The difficulty in establishing the role of RTW in a state's economic performance can be seen in a frequently cited 1998 study by Holmes that analyzed manufacturing employment in counties along several state borders in which one state was an RTW state (termed "probusiness" in the study) and the other was a union security state (termed "antibusiness" in the study).[28] The author suggested that many local factors such as climate and access to transportation are similar on both sides of the border and that varied outcomes on either side of the border would reflect the respective policies of the states.

Table 4. Employment Levels for Right to Work and Union Security States, 2001, 2006, and 2011

	Employment (in thousands)			Change in Employment		
	2001	2006	2011	2001-2006	2006-2011	2001-2011
Total	131,590	135,836	131,336	3.2%	-3.3%	-0.2%
RTW States	49,797	52,918	51,574	6.3%	-2.5%	3.6%
Union Security States	81,793	82,918	79,762	1.4%	-3.8%	-2.5%

Source: Annual averages from the Bureau of Labor Statistics' Current Employment Statistics, generated at http://www.bls.gov/sae/#data. In this presentation, CRS has divided the data into RTW and union security states.

Notes: Due to varied data sources, employment levels may not be directly comparable to other tables. Total employment was determined by calculating the sum of states. In accordance with its status through 2011, Indiana was classified as a union security state.

The study tracked growth in manufacturing employment between 1947 (the passage of the Taft- Hartley Act) and 1992. It found that among counties within 25 miles of a state border, manufacturing employment in counties in RTW states grew about one-third faster than manufacturing employment in the nearby counties in non-RTW states.

The author concluded that the abrupt changes in employment at the state borders were consistent with the hypothesis that state policies influence site location.

In spite of these findings, the author expressed uncertainty as to the influence of RTW laws. Holmes emphasized that while he used RTW and union security as a proxy for states' business- friendliness, "the effect found here is an *overall* effect of state policy. The analysis does not identify the contribution to the overall effect of any one particular policy, for example, a right-to- work law" (emphasis in original).

Holmes further qualified the study's findings regarding RTW by citing a ranking of states' business climates. He noted that while RTW laws were only one of 15 equally-weighted criteria considered in the ranking, 14 of the 15 highest-ranked states had an RTW law, suggesting a strong correlation between RTW laws and other pro-business policies.

Holmes concluded that subsequent study is necessary to isolate the effect of RTW laws. CRS was unable to locate such a study, and given the frequency with which the Holmes study is still cited in RTW discussions, it appears that no such widely accepted study has emerged.

Right to Work and Wages

Table 5 presents average annual wage data from RTW and union security states in 2011 and shows that wages in union security states were 16.6% higher than in RTW states. As is the case with employment levels, there is little controversy over these aggregate numbers and the trend depicted in the table is relatively well-established.

Many studies have attempted to control for differences between the states and isolate the effect of RTW polices. A 1998 summary of the empirical literature concluded that "RTW laws have no impact on union wages, nonunion wages, or average wages in either the public or private sector."[29] Subsequent studies have challenged this conclusion, with findings mixed between positive and negative wage effects from RTW laws.

A 2011 study by Gould and Shierholz examined household survey data to compare wages between RTW and union security states while controlling for personal characteristics (such as the lower share of workers in RTW states with college degrees) as well as macro state characteristics (such as the higher cost of living in union security states).[30]

In total, the study controlled for 42 demographic, economic, geographic, and policy factors. The study concluded that "[o]nce we control for our comprehensive set of both individual and state-level observable characteristics, we find that the mean effect of working in a right-to-work state is a 3.2% reduction in wages." The same study reached similar conclusions regarding negative relationships between RTW and employed-provided benefits.

Another study with a very different methodology challenges this conclusion. A 2003 study by Reed examined state-level income data and, unlike many other studies, controlled for the states' varied economic conditions before the adoption of RTW.[31]

Among other variables, Reed controlled for each state's per capita income in 1945, prior to the initial wave of RTW laws following the passage of the Taft-Hartley Act.

The author reasoned that since RTW states were typically among the lower-income states at the time of enacting RTW, comparisons between RTW and union security states should control for this initial condition. The study concluded that, after controlling for income levels in 1945, RTW laws were related to wages 6.7% higher than in union security states.

The study also concluded that this effect was strongest in states with the lowest levels of income in 1945 and that states with higher initial incomes experienced weaker or perhaps even negative effects from RTW laws.

Right to Work and Other Outcomes

Additional RTW-related research on other topics further illustrates the difficulty of comprehensively evaluating the effects of RTW policies. For example, Zullo examined fatal on- the-job injuries of construction workers in the context of RTW laws and union density.

The study concluded that higher unionization rates in the local construction industry were related to lower fatality rates and that unionization's relationship with reducing fatalities was strongest in union security states.[32]

Conversely, studies that considered other outcomes suggested benefits to RTW laws. A 2009 study by Stevans found that RTW had little effect on employment but did have a positive relationship with proprietors' incomes.[33] A 2000 study looked at the performance of stocks for companies based in Louisiana and Idaho during the periods when those states were initially passing their RTW laws in 1976 and 1986, respectively.

This study evaluated the performance of these stocks on days where there was key movement in RTW legislation in the respective states and found that, relative to the larger market, stocks from companies based in these states increased 2% to 4%.[34]

Table 5. Employment and Average Annual Wages in Right to Work and Union Security States, 2011

	Employment	Total Wages (in thousands)	Average Annual Wage
United States	**129,411,099**	**6,217,285,908**	**$48,043**
RTW States	50,579,217	2,207,308,191	43,641
Union Security States	78,831,882	4,009,977,717	50,867

Source: Bureau of Labor Statistics, Quarterly Census of Employment and Wages (QCEW). In this presentation, CRS has divided the data into RTW and union security states.

Note: Due to varied data sources, employment levels may not be directly comparable to other tables. In accordance with its status in 2011, Indiana was classified as a union security state.

CONSIDERATIONS FOR A NATIONAL RIGHT TO WORK LAW

The primary issue in the ongoing RTW debate pertains to the rights and expectations of workers who are covered by a collective bargaining agreement but do not wish to pay union dues. Supporters of expanding RTW laws argue that these workers should have a right to choose whether or not to support their representing labor organization. Advocates of union security agreements emphasize that negotiating labor organizations are required to represent all workers in the bargaining unit, so it is a reasonable expectation to require all workers in the bargaining unit to financially support the labor organization.

Advocates and opponents of expanding RTW laws also posit higher-order effects to support their respective views. Supporters of RTW laws suggest that such laws increase employer flexibility, and may make it difficult for strong unions to be sustained, which in turn may lead to increases in efficiency and economic output. Opponents of RTW laws suggest that such laws reduce the financial viability of unions, leading to declines in collective bargaining and corresponding benefits for workers.

In assessing the potential effects of expanding RTW, existing empirical research is inconclusive. Comparing outcomes in states with and without RTW laws can provide limited perspectives on possible effects of these laws, but states' economies are extremely complex and even the most sophisticated studies are unable to fully isolate the effects of varied union security policies.

Furthermore, the variation in findings among researchers suggests that no consensus will be reached in the near future. As such, the ongoing debate on RTW may be driven by factors other than rigorous empirical evidence.

End Notes

[1] See 29 U.S.C. 158(a)(3). Specifically, the NLRA states that contracts with union security agreements may require all covered workers to be members of the negotiating labor organization within 30 days of beginning employment. The courts have interpreted union membership to be equivalent to paying union dues. This distinction is outlined in greater detail in the "Union Security Agreements and Required Union Dues" section of this report.

[2] Bruce Feldracker, *Labor Guide to Labor Law*, 4th ed. (2000), pp. 1-3.

[3] For a detailed discussion of the NLRA and related laws, see CRS Report R42526, *Federal Labor Relations Statutes: An Overview*.

[4] The NLRA, as amended, is at 29 U.S.C. 141-197. It does not cover private sector workers employed by railroads or airlines; these workers are covered by the aforementioned Railway Labor Act.

[5] See P.L. 74-198, Section 1.

[6] See 29 U.S.C. 164(b). The RTW provisions of the NLRA are also sometimes referred to as 14(b) provisions, after the section of the NLRA that permits RTW laws.

[7] See P.L. 86-257.

[8] See P.L. 96-593.

[9] Covered workers in the construction industry can be required to become union members within seven days, see 29 U.S.C. 158(f).

[10] See *NLRB v. General Motors Corporation*, 373 U.S. 734 (1963).

[11] Bruce Feldacker, *Labor Guide to Labor Law*, Fourth ed. (2000), pp. 424-438.

[12] See 29 U.S.C. 169.

[13] The RLA also applies to any company that is defined as a "carrier" by 45 USC 151, first paragraph. It also includes any company that is controlled by a railroad or airline.

[14] See 45 U.S.C. 152, paragraph eleventh.

[15] See 39 U.S.C. 1205.

[16] The Government Accountability Office (GAO) is excluded from FSLMRS coverage, but the General Accounting Office Personnel Act of 1980 gave GAO employees the right to organize and bargain collectively.

[17] See 5 U.S.C. 7115.

[18] See Section 1 of Indiana Code 22-6-6.

[19] See *Local 514 Transport Workers Union v. Keating*, Oklahoma supreme court (2003) and 10th Circuit Court (2004).

[20] For example, in the 112th Congress, H.R. 2040 had 77 cosponsors and S. 2173 had 19 cosponsors.

[21] For example, see H.R. 2775 in the 112th Congress.

[22] For one discussion with empirical examples, see William J. Moore, "The Determinants and Effects of Right-to-Work Laws: A Review of the Recent Literature," *Journal of Labor Economics*, Summer 1998, pp. 449-50.

[23] Russel Sobel, "Empirical Evidence on the Union Free Rider Problem: Do Right-to-Work Laws Matter?," *Journal of Labor Research*, Summer 1995, pp. 347-365.

[24] David Ellwood and Glenn Fine, "The Impact of Right to Work Laws on Union Organizing," *Journal of Political Economy*, April 1987, pp. 250-273.

[25] For representative example, see National Institute for Labor Relations Research, *Right to Work States Benefit from Faster Growth, Higher Real Purchasing Power - 2011 Update*, October 25, 2011, http://nilrr.org/2011/10/25/right- work-states-benefit-faster-growth-higher-real-purchasing-power-2011-update/.

[26] For a representative critique, see Gordon Lafer and Sylvia Allegretto, *Does Right to Work Create Jobs?: Answers from Oklahoma*, Economic Policy Institute, March 16, 2011, http://www.epi.org/publication/bp300/.

[27] For a summary of incentives for businesses in North Dakota, see "Quick Facts," from the North Dakota Department of Commerce, Division of Economic Development and Finance at http://www.business.nd.gov/uploads/resources/203/2010quickfactsbrochureprint.pdf.

[28] Thomas Holmes, "The Effect of State Policies on the Location of Manufacturing: Evidence from State Borders," *Journal of Political Economy*, vol. 106, no. 4 (August 1998), pp. 667-705.

[29] William J. Moore, "The Determinants and Effects of Right-to-Work Laws: A Review of the Recent Literature," *Journal of Labor Economics*, Summer 1998, p. 460.

[30] See Heidi Shierholz and Elise Gould, *The Compensation Penalty of "Right-to-Work" Laws*, Economic Policy Institute, Issue Brief #299, February 17, 2011, http://www.epi.org/publication/bp299/.

[31] Robert W. Reed, "How Right to Work Laws Affect Wages," *Journal of Labor Research*, Fall 2003.

[32] Roland Zullo, *Right-to-Wok Laws and Fatalities in Construction*, University of Michigan Institute for Research of Labor, Employment, and the Economy, March 2011, http://irlee.umich.edu/Publications/Docs/ RightToWorkLawsAndFatalitiesInConstruction.pdf.

[33] Lonnie K. Stevans, "The Effect of Endogenous Right-to-Work Laws on Business and Economic Conditions in the United States: A Multivariate Approach," *Review of Law and Economics*, 2009, pp. 595-614.

[34] Steven Abraham and Paula Voos, "Right to Work Laws: New Evidence from the Stock Market," *Southern Economic Journal*, October 2000, pp. 345-362.

In: Right to Work Laws …
Editor: Morgan N. Broderick

ISBN: 978-1-62417-918-1

Chapter 2

FEDERAL LABOR RELATIONS STATUTES: AN OVERVIEW*

Alexandra Hegji

SUMMARY

Since 1926, Congress has enacted three major laws that govern labor-management relations for private sector and federal employees. An issue for Congress is the effect of these laws on employers, workers, and the nation's economy. The Bureau of Labor Statistics estimates that, nationwide, 14.8 million employees are union members. In the 112th Congress alone, more than 30 bills were introduced to amend federal labor relations statutes. The proposals ranged from making union recognition without a secret ballot election illegal to further modifying runoff election procedures. These legislative activities, and the significant number of employees affected by federal labor relations laws, illustrate the current relevance of labor relations issues to legislators and their constituents.

The three major labor relations statutes in the United States are the Railway Labor Act, the National Labor Relations Act, and the Federal Service Labor-Management Relations Statute. Each law governs a distinct population of the U.S. workforce.

---

* This is an edited, reformatted and augmented version of the Congressional Research Service Publication, CRS Report for Congress R42526, dated November 26, 2012.

The Railway Labor Act (RLA) was enacted in 1926, and its coverage extends to railway and airline carriers, unions, and employees of the carriers. The RLA guarantees employees the right to organize and collectively bargain with their employers over conditions of work and protects them against unfair employer and union practices. It lays out specific procedures for selecting employee representatives and provides a dispute resolution system that aims to efficiently resolve labor disputes between parties, with an emphasis on mediation and arbitration. The RLA provides multiple processes for dispute resolution, depending on whether the dispute is based on a collective bargaining issue or the application of an existing collective bargaining agreement.

The National Labor Relations Act (NLRA) was enacted in 1935. The NLRA's coverage extends to most other private sector businesses that are not covered by the RLA. Like the RLA, the NLRA guarantees employees the right to organize and collectively bargain over conditions of employment and protects them against unfair employer and union activities. However, its dispute resolution system differs from the RLA's in that it is arguably more adversarial in nature; many disputes are resolved through adjudication, rather than through mediation and arbitration.

The Federal Service Labor-Management Relations Statute (FSLMRS) was enacted in 1978, and its coverage extends to most federal employees. The basic framework of the FSLMRS is similar to that of the NLRA; however, employee rights are more restricted under the FSLMRS, given the unique nature of their employer, the federal government. Federal employees have the right to organize and collectively bargain, but they cannot bargain over wages or strike. Additionally, the President has the power to unilaterally exclude an agency or subdivision from coverage under the FSLMRS if he determines that its primary work concerns national security.

This report provides a brief history and overview of the aims of each of these statutes. It also discusses key statutory provisions for each statute.

Congress has enacted three major laws that govern labor-management relations. The first law, the Railway Labor Act (RLA), was enacted in 1926. The RLA applies to railway and airline carriers. In 1935, Congress passed the National Labor Relations Act (NLRA), which applies to private sector employers other than railroad and airline carriers, and in 1978, Congress enacted the Federal Service Labor-Management Relations Statute (FSLMRS), which applies to most federal employees. This report provides an overview of these three labor relations laws by giving a brief history of each law and discussing how each statute operates and is administered.

This report uses specific "terms of art" relevant to these acts. Appendix A defines these "terms of art." Appendix B provides a list of acronyms used in this report. Appendix C contains a table that compares provisions of all three laws.

THE RAILWAY LABOR ACT

Background

By the late 19th Century, the railroad industry had a significant impact on the U.S. economy. It helped connect the coasts, making settlement of the western United States much easier. Farmers were able to ship their goods to cities hundreds of miles away, and consumers were able to purchase products made in factories across the nation.[1] The railroad industry was also a major consumer of U.S. goods. It used over 75% of the steel produced in the United States, a large portion of the United States' extracted coal, and was the nation's primary employer.[2]

As the public began to depend on railroads and their regular availability, railroad workers also began to unionize.[3] Because the nation grew dependent on railroads, labor-management disputes that grew into work stoppages adversely affected the nation's welfare.

Enacted in 1926, the Railway Labor Act (RLA) continued a pattern of federal attempts at regulating labor relations in the industry.[4] It was the product of an agreement between industry and labor that Congress adopted. The act was intended to help maintain labor-management peace within the railway industry and thereby avoid work stoppages that could carry with them adverse economic and social effects.[5] The act's five major purposes are to:

- prevent any interruption to commerce or to the operation of any carrier;
- ensure employees the right to organize or join a labor union;
- ensure railway carriers and employees the right to select bargaining representatives without interference from the other party;
- provide timely settlement of disputes over rates of pay, rules, or working conditions; and
- provide timely settlement of disputes growing out of grievances or over interpretation or application of existing union contracts.[6]

To accomplish these goals, Congress established a system based on collective bargaining between labor and management, relying on mediation facilitated by the newly created National Mediation Board (NMB) and voluntary arbitration if neither collective bargaining nor mediation worked.

Major Amendments

1934 Amendments

The original RLA called for parties to establish by agreement special adjustment boards (SBAs) to resolve disputes over contract interpretation or application concerning changes in rates of pay, rules, or working conditions. These boards could be national, regional, or local in scope and would typically be composed of an equal number of carrier and employee representatives. If an adjustment board was unable to resolve a dispute because of a deadlock, the dispute could be referred to the Board of Mediation.[7] In the 1934 amendments, Congress created the National Railroad Adjustment Board (NRAB), which has jurisdiction over contract interpretation and administration disputes that cannot be resolved through direct negotiations. If the NRAB is deadlocked, it selects a referee to make an award in the dispute.[8] A referee is a neutral person who sits with the NRAB as a member and makes an award in the dispute at issue. Additionally, Congress replaced the Board of Mediation with the NMB, which can resolve disputes between parties concerning changes in rates of pay, rules, working conditions, and any other dispute not referable to NRAB.

Congress also strengthened the RLA's provisions that allow carriers and employees to select representatives freely and without interference from each other. It added language specifically stating that employees have the right to organize and collectively bargain and added a provision requiring that a majority of employees in a craft or class must support a union before it is recognized as their representative. Additionally, the amendments prohibited carriers from denying or questioning an employee's right to organize or join a union and tasked the NMB with investigating representation disputes. The amendments also provided for both civil and criminal means to enforce the RLA's provisions.[9]

Congress explicitly prohibited carriers from unilaterally changing pay rates, rules, and working conditions and added a "status quo" provision, which prohibits changes to pay rates, rules, and working conditions for 30 days after parties are released from the NMB's services.[10] Finally, the definition of "carrier" was broadened to include companies that perform operations integral to railway transportation but not already covered by the act.[11]

1936 Amendments

In 1936, Congress extended most of the RLA's provisions to commercial airline carriers that operate in interstate or foreign commerce and airlines that transport mail for, or under contract with, the U.S. government.[12] Although the airline industry was relatively new in 1936, Congress acknowledged that it was part of the national transportation system that was vital to the economic well-being of the nation and that it too would need mechanisms to assist in dispute resolution and avoiding work stoppages. While the National Labor Relations Act (NLRA) was enacted in 1935 and covered most private sector employees, labor wanted airline carriers to be included under the RLA, because it believed the RLA's mediation/arbitration dispute resolution mechanisms provided more flexibility for the constantly changing, fledging industry.[13]

Additional Amendments

Between 1951 and 1981, the RLA was the subject of much congressional action. The major changes enacted are discussed below. This is followed by a depiction of the NLRA provisions currently in effect.

1951 Amendments

In 1951, Congress amended the RLA to allow carriers and unions to enter into union security agreements. These agreements require employees to pay union dues equal to the cost of representation as a condition of employment. However, under a union security agreement, employees are not required to become formal members of the union. State right-to-work laws that prohibit or restrict union security agreements are preempted by the RLA.[14]

1966 and 1981 Amendments

In 1966, Congress amended the RLA to provide for Public Law Boards (PLBs) that can be established upon the request of either party. Unlike an SBA, the parties do not need to agree on the creation of a PLB. PLBs are composed of one person selected by the carrier and one person selected by the union. Each selected board member is compensated by the carrier or union who selected them. If these selected board members deadlock on an issue, they designate a neutral third party to decide the dispute. If the selected board members are unable to agree on a neutral party, the NMB designates the neutral party. The neutral party is compensated by the NMB.[15] Finally, in 1981, Congress established emergency procedures for certain publicly funded and operated carriers that provide commuter rail services.[16]

FAA Modernization and Reform Act of 2012

The RLA was most recently amended in 2012 during the 112th Congress as part of the Federal Aviation Administration (FAA) Modernization and Reform Act of 2012. Under these amendments, for the NMB to conduct an election or otherwise certify a union for a craft of unrepresented employees, the NMB must receive, along with an application for certification, authorization cards signed by at least 50% of the employees in the craft or class seeking representation. Before this amendment, those parties filing an application for certification were required to include authorization cards signed by 35% of employees in the craft or class seeking representation.[17]

The 2012 amendments also changed the rules for runoff elections. Previously, only the names of the two unions that received the most votes in the first election were on the runoff ballot. If more employees voted not to have a union than voted for one or both of the unions that received the most votes, the runoff ballot did not include the choice of not being represented by a union.[18] Under the 2012 amendments, the runoff ballot has the two choices, including the choice not to be represented, that received the most votes in the initial election.[19]

The 2012 amendments also mandated periodic NMB evaluations and audits.[20]

Overview

The RLA seeks to prevent labor-management disputes that could interrupt railroad and airline service and harm the economy. It grants certain rights to both workers and carriers, seeks to prevent practices that could frustrate a peaceful worker-carrier relationship, and provides mechanisms for workers and carriers to resolve disputes.

To achieve these goals, the RLA regulates the labor-management relationship between workers and carriers in the railway and airline industries. It provides parties with a standard process for choosing a union to act as an employee representative in the collective bargaining process and details which individuals can participate in the process. Once a union is selected, the RLA governs which subjects workers and unions can negotiate. The RLA also regulates how workers, carriers, and unions should behave towards each other during the union selection and collective bargaining processes and prohibits certain unfair actions.

The RLA provides for several entities to administer and enforce its provisions. The National Mediation Board (NMB) is the primary agency charged with administration and enforcement of the act and also provides mediation service to parties who cannot reach a resolution in a dispute. The National Railway Adjustment Board (NRAB) is an NMB tribunal that hears and decides (arbitrates) grievances in the railway industry. Additionally, the RLA allows parties to a dispute in the railway industry to establish their own arbitration tribunals, known as Special Boards of Adjustment (SBAs), or a single party to request that the NMB create a Public Law Board (PLB) to arbitrate its dispute. Various System Boards of Adjustment (System Boards), created jointly by labor and management, arbitrate disputes in the airline carrier industry. Finally, if an unresolved dispute threatens to substantially interrupt commerce, the President can create a Presidential Emergency Board (PEB) to investigate and aid in the resolution of the dispute.

Scope of Coverage

The RLA regulates the collective bargaining rights and duties of carriers and employees in the railway and airline carrier industries. "Collective bargaining" refers to the process of negotiation between these parties regarding working conditions. Employers are referred to as "carriers" in the RLA. The term "carrier" is used throughout this discussion for consistency with the act. The preliminary sections of the act define "carrier" and "employee," and those definitions are used to determine who is covered by the act and its accompanying regulations.

Carrier Defined

Under the RLA, a carrier is defined as:

> any company which is directly or indirectly owned or controlled by or under common control with any carrier by railroad and which operates any equipment or facilities or performs any service (other than trucking service) in connection with the transportation, receipt, delivery, elevation, transfer in transit, refrigeration or icing, storage, and handling of property transported by railroad, and any receiver, trustee, or other individual or

body, judicial or otherwise, when in the possession of the business of any such "carrier"[21]

In addition to railroads, later adopted provisions cover airline carriers. The RLA also applies to any company that is directly or indirectly controlled by, or under common control with, a railroad or airline carrier that falls under the coverage of the act.

The RLA specifically excludes "trucking service" and most "street, interurban, or suburban electric railways" from its scope. However, if a trucking company almost exclusively performs services for a rail carrier, the trucking exemption may not apply.[22]

Employee Defined

The RLA defines an employee as any "person in the service of a carrier ... who performs any work defined as that of an employee or subordinate official."[23] Temporary, probationary and furloughed employees generally are within the RLA's definition of "employee."[24]

Rights and Duties under the Law

The act both mandates and prohibits certain actions of all parties involved in a labor-management dispute. The act grants employees the right to organize and collectively bargain. It also sets forth the procedures and standards to be applied in the selection of a union as an employee representative and the subsequent relations between the union, the carrier, and the employees.

Employees can select a union that will represent their craft or class's interests in bargaining with carriers over working conditions. A craft or class is a group of employees who are or wish to be represented by a union. A union can be recognized as a representative through either a secret ballot election or voluntary carrier recognition.

Certain conduct is prohibited in the carrier-union-employee relationship. Carriers and unions cannot interfere with employees' right to organize and select a union representative. Carriers can only bargain with the employee-selected union, and the parties cannot use self-help until they have reached an impasse in negotiations and have exhausted all of the RLA's dispute resolution mechanisms. Self-help is a way in which one party can exert pressure on the other party and occurs outside of the formal dispute resolution process. For example, strikes and worker lockouts are forms of self-help.

Union Selection

The RLA specifically states that employees have a right to select a union free from carrier interference or influence. A majority of a craft or class determines the union to represent that craft or class.[25] The NMB has exclusive jurisdiction to certify unions. A union can be certified as an employee representative if at least one party to a representation dispute petitions the NMB to conduct a secret ballot election and the union receives a majority of votes cast. However, the NMB will recognize the validity of a carrier-union agreement under which a carrier voluntarily recognizes a union as an employee representative. The NMB also has exclusive jurisdiction to determine a craft or class of employees, and this decision is practically unreviewable by courts.[26]

Determination of a Craft or Class

In defining a class or craft, the NMB will consider many factors including historical or traditional crafts and similarity of job functions between employees.[27] The NMB generally adheres to the traditional railroad craft or class distinctions.[28] When Congress extended coverage of the RLA to airlines, the industry was relatively new and did not have historical crafts. However, over the years, the NMB has come to distinguish several crafts within the industry.[29]

A union may only be certified on a system-wide basis. Union certification extends to members of that craft throughout the carrier's organization. The craft or class must include all employees who are eligible to be in the craft or class, including those at different locations.[30]

Eligibility to Vote in a Secret Ballot Election

Employees who regularly work in a craft or class are eligible to vote in a secret ballot election.[31] Employees who are furloughed, on a leave of absence, or probationary are eligible to vote. Contractors, retirees, and managers are ineligible to vote. Part-time, temporary, and dismissed employees may be eligible to vote, and the determination is made on a case-by-case basis.[32]

Certification

To determine a union, the NMB can conduct elections or use "any [other] appropriate method."[33]

Before the NMB selects a method to determine a union, it must complete an investigation to determine whether a representation dispute exists. To begin the investigation process, either party can petition for an investigation. The petition must be supported by a showing of interest in which a majority of workers in the craft or class involved sign authorization cards.[34] An NMB investigator compares the authorization cards with the list of system-wide, potential eligible voters provided by the carrier to determine if a sufficient percentage of authorization cards was submitted.

An investigator reports his findings to the NMB's General Counsel (see discussion of "RLA Enforcement and Adjudication Processes" below). If an investigator finds that a dispute exists, the General Counsel will establish the way in which the dispute will be resolved (e.g., secret ballot election).[35]

The NMB may conduct elections by mail, telephone, Internet, or in-person ballot. A union must receive a *majority of votes cast* to be certified by the NMB as the employees' bargaining representative. In 2010, this rule replaced a 75-year-long NMB practice that required that a *majority of workers vote* for representation before a union was certified.

The former practice effectively counted all those workers who did not vote in the election as "no union" votes. Now, an employee who does not vote is no longer counted in the vote tally. [36] If no choice receives a majority of the votes, the NMB may conduct a runoff election between the two choices that receive the most votes.[37]

The RLA does not preclude a carrier from voluntarily recognizing a union as an employee representative. If employees are unrepresented, the union seeking certification is the only organization involved, and the parties agree in writing, the NMB can certify the union based solely on the union's presenting authorization cards signed by a majority of employees in the craft.[38]

However, if the union is for a group of employees not generally recognized as a craft or class or if the craft or class is not represented system-wide, the voluntary recognition does not control the NMB's determination in a later representation dispute.[39]

Decertification

A union can have its certification revoked through decertification. The NMB does not have a formal procedure for decertifying a union, but has several practices that effectively remove an incumbent union's certification.[40] A union will be decertified when an individual or union petitions for a secret ballot election and less than 50% of voting employees cast ballots for the incumbent union or when the existing union freely renounces its certification.[41]

Bargaining Subjects

The RLA expressly mandates that all carriers and employees use "every reasonable effort" to create and maintain agreements on pay rates, rules, and working conditions and to settle all disputes arising out of such agreements (known as "direct negotiations").[42]

Prohibited Conduct

The RLA does not specifically list the unfair labor practices that it prohibits. Instead, the NMB looks to general considerations of fair dealing in defining the few bounds that the RLA does set. "Fair dealing" includes both unions' and carriers' responsibility to bargain in good faith, to recognize and respect each parties' representatives and concerns, and to refrain from interfering with each parties' rights.[43]

During Union Organization Efforts

The act protects employees' right to organize by prohibiting "interference, influence, or coercion by either party over the designation of representatives by the other."[44] Carriers may not deny or question an employee's right to organize, and carriers cannot use funds to maintain or assist a union in carrying out its duties or to influence an employee to leave or remain in a union.[45] Carriers cannot require prospective employees to sign an agreement to join or not to join a union.[46] Any carrier who willfully violates any of these provisions may be subject to civil and criminal penalties.[47] Additionally, the NMB can order rerun elections to eliminate the potential effects of any interference.[48]

During an Ongoing Carrier-Union Relationship

After certification of a union, carriers have the duty to bargain with that union.[49] A carrier has the duty to bargain only with the union and not directly with employees. Carriers cannot engage in direct communications with employees that give the impression that a carrier is unwilling to negotiate or communications that may disrupt negotiations or destroy a union's bargaining powers.[50]

During Self-Help

Self-help is the way in which one party can exert pressure on the other party and occurs outside of the formal dispute resolution process. Self-help includes peaceful striking, picketing, and locking out employees. Parties may not engage in self-help until they have exhausted the RLA's dispute resolution mechanisms; any self-help used afterwards must be lawful. Among the permissible actions employees can take are peaceful picketing, intermittent striking, and selective striking.

Additionally, employees may be able to engage in "secondary activity," through which they exert pressure on an entity with which they do not have a dispute.[51]

A carrier may hire permanent replacements for striking employees and keep those replacements at the end of the strike. However, a carrier may not discharge or eliminate the jobs of striking employees as retaliation for a strike.[52] A court has the ability to order parties to stop self-help (i.e., issue an injunction), if it finds that a carrier or a union has violated the status quo (i.e., neither party can change the current practices under an agreement).[53]

RLA Enforcement and Adjudication Processes

The RLA established several entities to administer and enforce the act. The National Mediation Board (NMB) is the primary agency charged with administration and enforcement and also provides mediation services to parties to a dispute. The National Railroad Adjustment Board (NRAB) is a tribunal under the NMB that hears and decides (arbitrates) grievances in the railway industry. Alternatively, parties in the railway industry can create their own arbitration tribunals, known as Special Boards of Adjustment (SBAs), or a single party can request that the NMB create a Public Law Board (PLB) to arbitrate the dispute. In the airline industry, various System Boards of Adjustment (System Boards), created jointly by labor and management, arbitrate disputes. The decisions of these entities can be reviewed by federal courts in limited circumstances.

National Mediation Board

The NMB is an independent agency that was created to administer and enforce the RLA. It is headed by a three member board. Each member serves full time and is appointed by the President and confirmed by the Senate for a term of three years. No more than two members can be of the same political party.[54] The three members self-designate a chairman on a yearly basis. The NMB has delegated its powers to investigate and adjudicate representation disputes to its General Counsel and oversees mediation and arbitration under the RLA.[55]

Adjustment Boards

The NRAB, SBAs, and System Boards are adjustment boards. An adjustment board is an entity that arbitrates disputes. Under the RLA, three types of adjustment boards exist for the railway industry (NRAB, SBAs, PLBs) and one exists for the airline carrier industry (System Boards).

The NRAB is a federal tribunal under the NMB that arbitrates grievances in the railroad industry. The NRAB consists of 34 members; seventeen are selected by carriers, and seventeen are selected by labor organizations of national scope.[56] The NRAB is divided into four divisions that generally operate independently of each other and process disputes involving specific types of employees.[57] Parties may seek compliance with NRAB decisions in federal district courts. District courts can also affirm or set aside, in whole or in part, NRAB orders.[58]

Alternatively, parties to a railway industry dispute can voluntarily agree to create an SBA, an arbitration tribunal. The NMB provides a list of potential arbitrators, known as the Roster of Arbitrators, to the parties, and the parties select the arbitrator from that list.

Finally, in the railway industry, a single party can request the establishment of a PLB to settle disputes for an individual railroad. Again, the parties choose arbitrators from the NMB's Roster of Arbitrators. The party upon whom the request is made must then enter into an agreement with the requesting party, establishing the board within 30 days of the request. If that party fails to agree to the creation of a PLB or fails to designate a member to the PLB, the requesting party may ask that the NMB designate an arbitrator.[59]

In all railway arbitration proceedings, the NMB pays the salaries and travel expenses of the arbitrators.[60]

When the RLA was amended to include airline carriers, it maintained the requirement of compulsory arbitration in certain disputes and established the National Air Transit Adjustment Board,[61] however, it was never created. Rather, airline carriers and unions created their own temporary special boards of adjustment, System Boards. Like railway carrier disputes, parties to an airline carrier dispute are required to engage in direct bargaining, but System Boards have no formal procedures and are limited in the jurisdiction agreed upon by the parties. System Boards must, therefore, look to collective bargaining agreements to determine how to proceed with a grievance.[62]

Unlike railway arbitration proceedings, the NMB does not pay the salaries and travel expenses to arbitrators in airline carrier industry disputes.[63]

Judicial Review

Grounds for judicial review and overturning either an NMB order or an adjustment board award are very narrow. A court can overturn an NMB order releasing parties from mediation if the order is outside of the NMB's jurisdiction or contrary to specific prohibitions in the RLA.[64]

Adjustment board awards may be reviewed and overturned if the award is affected by fraud, an adjustment board oversteps its jurisdiction, or the award does not conform to the RLA.[65] Additionally, an award can be called into question, referred to in the RLA as "impeached." To do so, a party must file a petition to impeach within 10 days of the final judgment. A decision can be impeached for several reasons: (1) if the award or proceedings do not conform to the substantive or procedural requirements of the RLA; (2) if the parties made a voluntary agreement to arbitrate and the award does not conform to the agreement; or (3) if a member of the board that rendered the award or a party to the arbitration was found guilty of fraud or corruption, and that fraud or corruption affected the outcome of the arbitration.[66]Any decision reached by an adjustment board is final and binding on the parties and can be enforced in the U.S. district courts.[67]

Dispute Resolution

Upon certification, a carrier has the duty to negotiate with, and only with, the certified union.[68] If parties fail to reach an agreement through direct negotiations, further RLA procedures may be invoked. The RLA divides disputes into two categories: major and minor disputes, and each type has its own dispute resolution mechanism. If a dispute cannot be resolved and the President believes that the dispute may substantially disrupt interstate commerce, he may invoke emergency procedures to resolve the dispute.

"Major" Disputes

"Major" disputes are those related to the process of collective bargaining (i.e., the parties cannot reach an agreement as to pay rates, rules, and working conditions). In the railway industry, agreements generally do not have expiration dates.[69] Rather, they become subject to change on a specified date within the original agreement. Major disputes, therefore, include both bargaining on the terms of an initial labor-management agreement and on any subsequent changes to the agreement the parties may wish to make.

Carriers and employees must give 30 days' written notice of any intended changes to the agreement to the other party. This is known as a "Section 6 notice." The parties must then agree on the time and place of a conference about the proposed changes within 10 days of receipt of the notice, and the conference between the parties must take place within the 30 days. Once the Section 6 notice has been served, each party must maintain the status quo.[70]

At any time during this direct bargaining process, either party may invoke the NMB's mediation services.[71] Parties continue to negotiate in the presence of an NMB mediator, and the mediator works with both parties, helping them to resolve their dispute. The NMB has sole discretion to decide when the parties can discontinue mediation because they have either reached an agreement or they are at an impasse and cannot reach an agreement.[72]

If the parties cannot reach an agreement, the NMB will "proffer arbitration" and invite the parties to submit their dispute to an arbitrator. This arbitration is voluntary-but-binding and is held before the appropriate adjustment board. If either or both parties refuse arbitration, the NMB sends written notice to the parties terminating its services. The parties then enter into a 30-day "cooling- off" period during which they cannot change the terms of the agreement.[73] After the cooling-off period, if the parties have not reached a mutual agreement, then they may exercise self-help, including strikes, lockouts, and imposition of new rules on the workforce.[74]

If parties do agree to arbitration, the arbitration board will comprise three members. Each party will select one arbitrator. These two arbitrators will then select a third. If the two arbitrators fail to select another within five days after their first meeting, the NMB will select the third arbitrator.[75] The arbitrators' decision is final as to all issues placed before them.[76]

"Minor" Disputes

A "minor" dispute is one involving the interpretation or application of an already existing agreement. As with major disputes, the parties have a duty to first engage in direct negotiations,[77] but, generally, a carrier may act on its own interpretation of the existing agreement while waiting for resolution of the dispute by an Adjustment Board.[78]

The RLA mandates that minor disputes be submitted to compulsory arbitration in front of the appropriate adjustment board, the NRAB for the railway industry and System Boards of Adjustment for airline carriers. In arbitration, members of the NRAB conduct hearings and make findings on the disputes. The parties must comply with the orders of the NRAB.[79]

Alternatively, the parties can mutually agree to form their own, temporary, adjustment board, a Special Board of Adjustment (SBA) that decides specific issues agreed upon by the parties. If one of the parties is dissatisfied with the SBA, it may give 90 days' notice to the other party to be brought under the jurisdiction of the NRAB or the System Boards of Adjustment.[80]

Finally, a single party can request of the other party that a PLB be created to resolve a dispute. The requesting party can select an arbitrator and if the other party does not agree to the establishment of a PLB or fails to select an arbitrator, the NMB will designate an arbitrator to sit on the PLB. If members of the PLB are unable to agree on an issue, they must select a neutral member of the board to decide the matter. If PLB members cannot agree on a neutral member within 10 days of their failure to agree on an issue, either member can request the NMB to appoint a neutral board member.[81]

Emergency Actions

Although a carrier and a union may exercise self-help at the end of the dispute resolution process, the NMB may determine that an unresolved dispute threatens "substantially to interrupt interstate commerce." It may then recommend that the President create a Presidential Emergency Board (PEB). The President may, in his discretion, create a PEB to investigate and issue a report on the dispute within 30 days of its creation. Parties must maintain the status quo upon the creation of a PEB and for the 30 days following the release of its report, unless the parties reach an agreement to the dispute.[82]

Publicly funded and operated commuter rails have a different set of PEB procedures. If the President decides not to create a PEB under the above mentioned procedures, parties to the dispute or the governor of a state through which the commuter rail runs may request that the President establish a PEB. If the parties have not settled within 60 days of the establishment of the PEB, the NMB is required to conduct a public hearing at which the parties explain why they have not accepted the PEB's dispute resolution recommendations. If the parties still have not reached a resolution 120 days after the PEB's creation, then any party or governor of a state through which the commuter rails run can request a second PEB. Upon such a request, the President must establish a second PEB. The parties must then submit to the NMB an offer for settlement within 30 days. The PEB than has 30 days to report to the President which offer it finds most reasonable. Throughout this process, parties may not engage in self-help.[83]

For both commuter and non-commuter rails, Congress may intervene (e.g., adopt PEB recommendations) in a dispute to prevent a work stoppage.

On several occasions, Congress has either created another study commission or adopted PEB recommendations, effectively imposing a new agreement on the parties.[84]

NATIONAL LABOR RELATIONS ACT

Background

In 1933, the United States was in the midst of the Great Depression. President Franklin D. Roosevelt and Congress pursued policies to stabilize a weak economy and reduce unemployment. To these ends, the National Industrial Recovery Act of 1933 (NIRA) was enacted, which guaranteed workers the right to organize and to collectively bargain. By enabling unions to exert pressure on employers to increase wages, Congress believed workers would spend their higher wages, thus increasing the nation's purchasing power.[85]

NIRA did not prohibit so-called company-dominated unions, unions that are organized or assisted by an employer to such an extent that they appear to be an employer's creation and not an employee bargaining representative. Also, some employers refused to recognize employee- selected unions, which prompted some employees to strike.[86] Ultimately, the U.S. Supreme Court declared that NIRA was unconstitutional. Congress then enacted the National Labor Relations Act (NLRA), which is often called the Wagner Act, after its Senate sponsor, Senator Robert Wagner. Unlike its predecessor, the Wagner Act prohibited company-dominated unions and established the majority rule principle for worker representation. The act proved more effective than NIRA in protecting and guaranteeing employee rights.[87]

Major Amendments

The Taft-Hartley Act

Although the Wagner Act, by many accounts, accomplished Congress's goals, some critiqued it as one-sided and believed it too heavily favored unions, enabling excessive union power and disrupting the labor-management equilibrium.[88] In 1947, Congress passed the Taft-Hartley Act, named after its sponsors Senator Robert Taft and Representative Fred Hartley. This act placed some restrictions on unions and guaranteed certain freedoms of conduct and speech to employers.

Specifically, the Taft-Hartley Act enumerated prohibited unfair labor practices for unions,[89] required unions to give notification before striking, prohibited closed shops,[90] and outlawed secondary boycotts.[91] The act allowed states to enact right-to-work laws and gave employers the right to request an election to determine which of multiple unions claiming to represent employees was in fact the employee representative.[92] Supervisors were prohibited from joining unions,[93] and employees were given the right to petition to decertify a union.[94] Additionally, Congress restructured the National Labor Relations Board (NLRB), the federal agency charged with enforcing the NLRA.[95]

The Landrum-Griffin Act

Ten years following the enactment of the Taft-Hartley Act, in response to allegations of union corruption, Congress passed the Labor Management Reporting and Disclosure Act of 1959, commonly called the Landrum-Griffin Act after its sponsors Representative Phillip Landrum and Senator Robert Griffin.[96] The act applies to parties covered under both the NLRA and the Railway Labor Act (RLA). It added a union member "Bill of Rights" that enumerated five basic rights of union members: equality of rights, safeguards against improper disciplinary actions, freedom of speech, freedom from interference with the right to sue, and freedom from increased dues except by majority vote. The act also increased internal union transparency by mandating that each union enact by-laws and issue yearly financial disclosures.[97] Additionally, the act set forth specific election procedures to help ensure that internal union elections were free of corruption.[98]

Overview

The NLRA seeks to prevent labor-management disputes that could burden or obstruct commerce and harm the economy. It grants certain rights to both workers and employers, seeks to prevent practices that could frustrate a peaceful worker-employer relationship, and provides mechanisms for workers and employers to resolve disputes.

To achieve these goals, the NLRA regulates the labor-management relationship between workers and employers in the private sector, excluding the railway and airline carrier industries. It provides parties with a standard process for choosing a union to act as an employee representative in the collective bargaining process and details which individuals can participate in the process. Once a union is selected, the NLRA governs which subjects workers and unions can negotiate. The NLRA also regulates how workers, employers, and unions should behave towards each other during the union selection and collective bargaining processes and prohibits certain unfair actions.

To administer and enforce the act, the NLRA established the National Labor Relations Board (NLRB). The NLRB investigates and adjudicates representation disputes, complaints of unfair labor practices (ULPs), and contract disputes. The NLRB's General Counsel investigates and prosecutes ULP claims, and the General Counsel has delegated its authority to issue ULP complaints to regional directors.

Additionally, the President has the ability to create a Presidential Emergency Board (PEB) to investigate and aid in dispute resolution when he believes that a threatened or actual strike or lockout will endanger national health.

Scope of Coverage

The NLRA regulates collective bargaining rights and duties for employers, employees, and unions in the private sector, excluding the railway and airline carrier industries. While commercial airline carriers fall under the RLA's jurisdiction, the aviation manufacturing (defense, space, and commercial) and general aviation (e.g., flight training, intercontinental jet transportation of executives and public officers) industries fall under the NLRA's jurisdiction.[99] As with the RLA, the NLRA's preliminary sections define "employer" and "employee," and those definitions determine who is covered by the act's regulations.

Employer Defined

The NLRB has jurisdiction over employers whose operations affect interstate commerce.[100] The NLRB can assert jurisdiction over any employer whose operations affect commerce. However, the NLRB has established administrative standards, limiting its jurisdiction to those cases involving employers with a substantial effect on commerce. If an employer meets these administrative standards, the NLRB *must* review the case. These standards are based on an employer's annual sales or gross revenue. For example, retailers must have annual sales of at least $500,000 and privately operated hospitals must have an annual revenue of at least $250,000.[101]

The NLRA's definition of employer includes any person "acting as an agent of an employer, directly or indirectly." This definition does not include the United States, a wholly owned government corporation, a state or its subdivisions, or any Federal Reserve Bank.[102] International organizations, while not specifically enumerated, are excluded from NLRA coverage.[103]

Employee Defined

An employee includes anyone who works for another for hire. Individuals who have stopped working because of a current labor dispute or unfair labor practice and who have not obtained equivalent employment are also included in the definition. Agricultural workers, domestic workers employed by a family or person within their home, individuals employed by their parent or spouse, independent contractors, and supervisors are not employees for the purposes of the NLRA.[104]

If a person does not fall under one of the excluded categories, he is assumed to be an employee under the act. Therefore, nonresident aliens and hospital resident physicians are considered employees. However, graduate students working in teaching positions and unpaid volunteers are not employees.[105]

A supervisor is not an employee. An individual is a supervisor if he has the authority to "hire, transfer, suspend, lay off, recall, promote, discharge, assign, reward, or discipline other employees, or responsibly direct them, or to adjust their grievances" and if that authority requires the use of independent judgment.[106] Individuals who are temporarily holding a supervisory position are usually considered employees and, therefore, afforded NLRA protections.[107] Managerial employees, although they may not exercise supervisory functions, are exempt from NLRA coverage because they "formulate and effectuate management policies" and have discretion in performing their jobs.[108]

Rights and Duties under the Law

The act both mandates and prohibits certain actions of all parties involved in a labor-management dispute. The act grants employees the right to organize and collectively bargain and sets forth the procedures and standards to be applied in the selection of a union as an employee representative and the subsequent relations between the union and the employer.

During organization, employees can select a union that will represent their bargaining unit's interests in bargaining with employers over working conditions. A bargaining unit is a group of employees who are or wish to be represented by a union. A union can be recognized as a representative through a union security agreement, a secret ballot election, or voluntary employer recognition.

Bargaining topics are divided into those that unions and employers must bargain over (mandatory subjects), those that parties may bargain over (permissive subjects), and those that parties are prohibited from bargaining over (illegal subjects).

Certain conduct is prohibited in the employer-union relationship during union organization and collective bargaining. Employers and unions cannot interfere with employees' right to organize and select a union. Employers and unions are required to bargain with each other in good faith over conditions of employment, and employers can only bargain with the employee-selected union. In limited circumstances, the parties can use some forms of self-help if they have reached an impasse in the bargaining process.

Union Selection

Employees have the right to choose their union representative.[109] A majority vote by the members of an appropriate bargaining unit determines the union.[110] A union must either be certified by the NLRB or voluntarily recognized by the employer before collective bargaining can begin.[111]

Union Security Agreements

Unions and employers are generally allowed to enter into union security agreements under which employees may be required, as a condition of employment, to become union members by paying dues and initiation fees. A job applicant cannot be required to be a union member for hiring consideration, but a newly hired employee can be required to become a dues-paying member on or 30 days after the start of employment. This type of union-security agreement is known as a union shop agreement. Agency shops may also be created. In an agency shop, employees who do not join the union pay a fee to the union for its services as a bargaining agent, in lieu of dues.[112]

The union's authority to enter into security agreements can be revoked if a majority of affected employees vote to do so. Only one deauthorization election per twelve-month period can be held. Petitions for deauthorization elections must be supported by at least 30% of employees in the affected bargaining unit. Any employees, including those not required to join the union by the terms of the collective bargaining agreement, but excluding supervisors, may petition for a deauthorization election.[113]

Most provisions of the NLRA preempt state law, however, the NLRA specifically allows states to enact "right-to-work" laws.[114] Right-to-work laws prohibit or restrict union security agreements and give employees the option of employment without requiring them to join a union or to pay union dues.[115]

Determination of a Bargaining Unit

A bargaining unit is a group of employees represented or seeking representation by a union. If a union and employer do not agree on an appropriate bargaining unit, the issue is settled by the NLRB.

A bargaining unit is generally determined on the basis of a "community of interest" of the employees involved and whether those employees can be reasonably grouped together. To determine a "community of interest," the NLRB will look to several factors including historical or traditional units; employee wishes; and whether employees have the same or similar interests with respect to pay rates, hours, and other working conditions. A bargaining unit may include the employees of one employer location or multiple employer locations; it may also include employees of multiple employers. A bargaining unit may include both professional and nonprofessional employees, however, a majority of professional employees must vote to be members of the unit.[116]

Eligibility to Vote in a Secret Ballot Election

Employees who work in the bargaining unit during the eligibility period set by the NLRB and who are employed at the time of an election may vote in an election. Employees who are on a leave of absence or furloughed are eligible to vote. Economic strikers[117] who have been replaced by permanent employees may be allowed to vote in elections held within 12 months after the beginning of the strike; their permanent replacements can vote in the same election.[118] Unfair labor practice strikers are entitled to vote in elections but their temporary replacements are not.[119]

Certification

A union can be recognized as an employee representative in a number of ways, including through a secret ballot election. To initiate a secret ballot election, an individual or union must file a representation petition with the

NLRB alleging that a "substantial number of employees" want union representation or that a recognized union no longer represents a majority of employees in the bargaining unit. An employer can also file a petition alleging that one or more organizations claim recognition. Petitions filed by employees or unions must be accompanied by authorization cards signed by at least 30% of employees.[120]

Consent Agreements

Before an election, the NLRB's regional staff will try to secure one of three types of consent- election agreement from the parties. Consent agreements are agreed upon by the parties and lay out the terms of an election, including which choices are to be included on the ballot and the method to determine voting eligibility.[121] A regional director of the NLRB must approve any consent-election agreement.[122] The three types of consent-election agreements are:

- **Pure consent agreement.** The parties agree to have the regional director resolve any disputes arising from the election, and the regional director's rulings are final.
- **Stipulated election agreement.** The regional director's rulings are subject to review by the adjudicatory arm of the NLRB.
- **Full consent agreement.** The parties agree that the regional director will resolve both pre- and post-election disputes.[123]

Each type of agreement usually gives the NLRB regional director the authority to conduct the election, but parties can agree to an election conducted by a third party, such as an arbitrator or a mediation board.[124]

NLRB-Administered Elections

If parties do not enter into a consent-election agreement, a formal representation hearing is held. The hearing provides a forum for the parties to present their arguments regarding the representation election and may include the examination of witnesses and introduction of evidence. After the hearing, the hearing officer gives a summary of the issues and evidence to the regional director and the regional director makes a decision on the issues.[125]

After the hearing, the NLRB can direct a secret ballot election. The NLRB can certify a union receiving the majority of votes cast in an election. If an election has more than one union on the ballot and no choice receives a majority of the vote, the two choices with the most votes face each other in a runoff election.[126]

Parties can file an objection to the election if they believe the NLRB's election standards have not been met. An election may be set aside if it was accompanied by interference with the employees' freedom of choice. Examples of interference with employee freedom of choice include threats of job or benefits loss, threats of violence, and incentives to influence an employee's vote.[127]

If a union is NLRB-certified, the employer must bargain with it in good faith for one year.[128]

Voluntary Recognition

The NLRA does not preclude employers from voluntarily recognizing a union as an employee representative. An employer may do this if a majority of employees in a bargaining unit have signed authorization cards. A union and employer can also enter into a card check agreement, under which an employer agrees to recognize a union before the union begins to collect authorization cards. A card check agreement may require the union to collect more than a majority of authorization cards from bargaining unit employees.[129]

If an employer voluntarily recognizes a union, employees can file a decertification petition or an election petition requesting representation by another union after a reasonable amount of time.

A reasonable amount of time is defined by the NLRA as at least six months, but no more than one year after the parties' first bargaining session.[130]

The NLRB may also require an employer to recognize and bargain with a union if a majority of employees signed authorization cards and the employer engaged in unfair labor practices that make a fair election unlikely.[131] The employer must bargain with the union, in good faith, for one year.[132]

Decertification

The NLRB requires a secret ballot election to decertify either certified or voluntarily recognized unions. A decertification petition may be filed by employees or a union acting on their behalf.

The petition must be signed by at least 30% of the employees in the bargaining unit represented by the union. Parties cannot file a decertification or election petition for unions certified in an NLRB- conducted election until one year after certification.[133]

Withdrawal of Recognition

Union recognition can be withdrawn under two circumstances. It can be withdrawn if

1. one year after certification the employer and union have not reached a contract agreement. Both parties must have bargained in good faith, and the employer must doubt that a majority of employees currently support the certified union. The employer's doubt must be based on objective information (e.g., a petition signed by a majority of employees), or
2. no contract agreement has been reached after a reasonable amount of time and the employer has a reasonable doubt, supported by objective information, that the union is no longer supported by a majority of unit employees.[134]

Bargaining Subjects

The NLRA mandates that employers must bargain with unions regarding "rates of pay, wages, hours of employment, and other conditions of employment."[135] Because the statute does not provide further explanation, the NLRB and courts have divided bargaining subjects into three distinct categories: mandatory, permissive, and illegal.

Mandatory Subjects

Mandatory bargaining subjects are those that "vitally affect" employees. Employers must bargain with unions over such subjects, are prohibited from taking unilateral action related to them, and cannot make agreements with individual union members about them.[136]

The NLRA defines the following terms: "wage," "hours of employment," and "other conditions of employment." The term "wage" includes

- overtime pay,
- shift differentials,
- paid holidays and vacations,
- commissions,
- severance pay,
- pensions,
- health insurance, and
- profit-sharing plans.

The term "hours of employment" includes work schedules. The term "other conditions of employment" include provisions for grievance procedures, workloads, and sick leave.[137]

Permissive Subjects

Permissive bargaining subjects are those that either party may propose for inclusion in collective bargaining but neither party is required to bargain over them. When a permissive subject is included in a collective bargaining agreement, that subject does not then become a mandatory subject. Permissive subjects include the definition of a bargaining unit, selection of bargaining representatives, and union-recognition clauses.[138]

Illegal Subjects

The NLRA specifically prohibits either party from requiring the other party to contract for provisions that are illegal or that go against Congress's intent in enacting the NLRA. Closed-shop and hot-cargo clauses are examples of such provisions.[139] Additional illegal subjects of bargaining include separation of employees by race, rules requiring preference for union members, and an employer's right to terminate and employee for union activity.[140]

Prohibited Conduct

The NLRA defines and prohibits certain conduct as unfair labor practices (ULPs) to protect the rights of both employees and employers.[141] Through its provisions, the NLRA attempts to prevent and remedy, but not punish, ULPs. The NLRB can issue cease-and-desist orders to stop ULPs, and it can require employers to reinstate and give back pay to employees who were improperly discharged for union activities.[142] A union may be required to give an employee back pay if it is responsible for a ULP that caused an employer to discharge a worker. Punitive damages, however, are generally unavailable.[143]

During Union Organization Efforts

The NLRA imposes restrictions on employers and unions during the process of union organization. The act prohibits employers and unions from interfering with or coercing employees exercising their right to organize.[144] The NLRB does not require a showing of intent to violate the act, rather, an employer's or union's conduct must tend to interfere with employees' right to organize.[145]

During union organization, neither an employer nor a union can threaten discharge, loss of benefits, or plant closure if employees exercise their right to organize. An employer cannot raise wages to discourage workers from unionizing or discriminate against employees regarding conditions of employment (e.g., give unfavorable work assignments), and a union cannot cause an employer to discriminate against employees regarding employment conditions.[146]

Employers are prohibited from dominating a union. An employer dominates a union when it has participated in the union's organization and assisted and supported its activities to such an extent that the union appears to be the employer's creation and not the employees' bargaining representative. Additionally, employers cannot interfere with or contribute money or other support to a union, such as supporting one union over another in an election or pressuring employees to financially support a union, absent a valid union security agreement.[147]

Unions are prohibited from interfering with employers' choice of selecting who will or will not represent them in the collective bargaining process.[148] A union cannot influence an employee's choice of representative in procedures to address individual employee complaints.[149]

During an Ongoing Employer-Union Relationship

Both employers and unions are required to bargain collectively and in good faith with one another over "wages, hours of employment, and other terms and conditions of employment."[150] "Good faith" has not been specifically defined, but factors surrounding the bargaining process are used to determine whether parties bargained in good faith, including the justification for proposals and a willingness to make concessions. Some actions, such as unilateral changes and bargaining directly with employees, are considered by the NLRB to be in and of themselves refusals to bargain and in violation of the requirement to bargain in good faith.[151]

Neither employers nor unions can "restrain or coerce employees" in exercising their right to bargain collectively.[152] Employers cannot discriminate against employees to encourage or discourage union membership or because they have filed charges or given testimony under the NLRA.[153] A union cannot cause an employer to discriminate against employees to encourage or discourage union membership.[154]

Unions can fine and discipline members, so long as those sanctions are consistent with NLRB policy. For instance, a union cannot fine, expel, or use violence against a member for filing a ULP charge, for testifying against other members in arbitration, or for refusing to participate in unlawful or unprotected activity. A union can, however, fine or suspend a member for violating internal union rules.[155]

During Self-Help

In certain situations, the NLRA protects employees when they exercise self-help. When self-help is protected, employers violate the act by taking adverse or discriminatory action against employees who are using self-help. Protected activities are those used by employees, in a peaceful manner, to exercise their rights under the act, such as certain economic strikes, sympathy strikes, filing grievances, and activity opposing union leadership.[156] Unprotected activities include those that are violent or unlawful. Unprotected employee activities include sit-down strikes, intermittent strikes, partial strikes, strikes in violation of a contract's no-strike clause, acts of disloyalty,[157] and disruptive or vulgar behavior.[158]

During a strike, employee rights differ depending on the reason for the strike. If the strike is economic, employees retain their employment status and cannot be discharged, but employers can replace them. After the strike, if the employer has hired replacements, the striking employees are not entitled to job reinstatement. However, if the striking employees cannot find regular and substantially equivalent work, they are entitled to be recalled by the employer to jobs for which they are qualified, when jobs become available.[159]

During a strike protesting an employer's unfair labor practices, employees can neither lose their job nor be permanently replaced. After the strike, absent serious misconduct[160] on their part, striking employees are entitled to return to their jobs.[161]

Employers can also engage in certain self-help activities. An employer can prevent employees from working (i.e., a lockout) but not over a dispute about non-mandatory bargaining subjects. During a strike, an employer can unilaterally establish employment terms and conditions for workers hired as striker replacements, but without a bargaining impasse, an employer may not alter employment terms and conditions of non-striking employees.[162]

NLRA Enforcement and Adjudication Processes

The NLRA established the National Labor Relations Board (NLRB) to administer and enforce the act. The NLRB has the power to investigate and adjudicate representation disputes, ULP complaints, and contract disputes.

NLRB decisions can be reviewed by federal courts in limited circumstances (see discussion below).

National Labor Relations Board

The NLRB is an independent federal agency charged with administering and enforcing the NLRA. It comprises a five-member Board and a General Counsel. Hereafter, the "NLRB" is used to refer to both the five-member Board and the General Counsel as a collective body. "The Board" refers to the five-member Board alone.

The Board and General Counsel are appointed by the President and confirmed by the Senate. Traditionally, the Board is comprised of two Democrats, two Republicans, and a fifth member who belongs to the same party as the President. If a position is vacant and the Senate is in recess, the President can make a "recess appointment." The appointment expires at the end of the next Senate session.[163]

The Board adjudicates objections and challenges to secret ballot elections, decides questions about the composition of bargaining units, and determines all ULP cases prosecuted by the General Counsel.[164] The General Counsel has authority over ULP investigations and the issuance of ULP complaints; it has delegated its authority to issue ULP complaints to 51 field offices, which are composed of approximately 1,680 full-time employees.[165]

Judicial Review

Only final orders issued by the Board in ULP cases are subject to judicial review by the courts.[166] Board orders do not have the force of law, and parties can only be compelled to comply with NLRB orders through the U.S. courts of appeals.[167]

Generally, U.S. district courts cannot review Board decisions on ULP or representation cases. District courts can review representation decisions in connection with the review of an order in a ULP case. District courts can review representation cases if the Board made an order in excess of its jurisdiction or contrary to a specific provision in the NLRA.[168] The Board and federal courts are not allowed to review General Counsel decisions not to issue a ULP complaint, unless they are in connection with a review of a Board final order.[169]

If, after an investigation, the regional director has "reasonable cause to believe" that the ULP charge is true and that a complaint should be issued, the regional director must petition the district court for appropriate relief.[170]

Dispute Resolution

Unfair Labor Practice Disputes

An employee, employer, union, or any other person can initiate a ULP investigation against an employer or a union by filing a charge with the NLRB no more than six months after the alleged incident.[171] The charge is then investigated by the regional director, and the regional director determines whether a formal complaint should be issued. A refusal to issue a complaint can be appealed to the General Counsel. However, parties do not have a right to Board or court review.[172]

If the General Counsel determines that a charge has merit, he may try to settle the matter either formally or informally. In an informal settlement, parties generally agree to withdraw the charge upon remedial action and notice of the proposed settlement terms to affected employees. If the charged party does not comply with the agreement terms, the settlement will be withdrawn, and the case will be prosecuted. The settlement is not subject to judicial review.[173]

Formal settlements are used in cases where the General Counsel finds a persistent or deliberate violation of the NLRA. In a formal settlement, the charged party agrees to the Board's issuing a formal remedial order. If the charged party violates the settlement, the NLRB may institute judicial proceedings, or the party may be held in contempt.[174]

When a settlement is not reached in a meritorious case, the regional office will issue a complaint. Hearings are then held before an administrative law judge (ALJ), who issues a decision and recommendations to the Board. If a party does not object to the ALJ's decision, the Board can adopt the ALJ's decision as its own. Otherwise, the Board can review the ALJ's decision and issue its own orders. The General Counsel is responsible for ensuring compliance with the Board's orders.[175]

Contract Disputes

Arbitration is the primary mechanism for resolving contract disputes. In arbitration, the union and employer present their positions to an arbitrator who resolves the dispute. When arbitration is not possible, a party can bring a suit for contract violations in either state or federal court. However, if state law regarding contract interpretation or substance contradicts federal law, federal law prevails.[176] The Board also has the authority to interpret collective bargaining contracts, but courts generally do not defer to the Board in contract interpretation.[177] Both courts and the Board can issue injunctions to prevent certain actions, such as strikes that are in breach of a no-strike contract clause that requires arbitration.[178]

Emergency Actions

When the President believes that a threatened or actual strike or lockout that affects an entire industry or a substantial part of it will endanger national health or safety, he or she may appoint a "board of inquiry" to investigate the issue. A board of inquiry can include a chairman and any other members the President chooses. The board then issues a report on the facts of the dispute to the President. However, the report cannot include recommendations.[179]

After a report is issued, the President may direct the Attorney General to petition a U.S. district court to order a party to end the strike or lockout. If the court finds that the activity does indeed affect at least a substantial portion of an industry and threatens national health or safety, it will order a party to end the strike or lockout. A district court's orders may be appealed to a federal court of appeals.[180]

While the injunction is in effect, the parties to the dispute are encouraged to settle the matter on their own, and the board of inquiry reconvenes. After 60 days, the board reports to the President the current state of relations between the parties. Within 15 days of the issuance of the report, the NLRB must then conduct a secret ballot election of the employees involved in the dispute on whether they wish to accept a final offer of settlement made by their employer.[181]

After either the certification of the secret ballot election or a settlement, the injunction is discharged. The President submits a report detailing the process and any other recommendations of appropriate action to Congress.[182]

THE FEDERAL SERVICE LABOR-MANAGEMENT RELATIONS STATUTE

Background

While many private sector employees gained statutory rights to collective bargaining and remedies to unfair labor practices throughout the 1920s and 1930s, many of their public counterparts remained unprotected until the 1960s.[183] Traditional concepts of government sovereignty and public employees' general satisfaction with their job security contributed to this disparity.[184] However, by the 1960s, many federal public employees found their jobs to be less secure due to organizational and technological changes. Moreover, many commentators thought the federal government's willingness to extend collective bargaining rights to private employees but not to its own employees was inconsistent.[185]

Executive Order 10988

Union recognition bills were introduced in each Congress throughout the 1950s, but both President Harry Truman and President Dwight Eisenhower strongly opposed them. In 1961, President John F. Kennedy formed the Task Force on Employee-Management Relations in the Federal Service, which evaluated and made recommendations about federal employee unionization. In 1962, President Kennedy implemented the Task Force recommendations through Executive Order 10988.[186] The order granted federal employees the right to join, or not to join, labor unions and to collectively bargain. These new rights, however, were not as extensive as those of private employees. For instance, federal employees could not negotiate over wages and were prohibited from striking. Additionally, an agency could require that employees negotiate over a collective bargaining agreement only during non-official time (i.e., at times when employees were not on duty and entitled to compensation).[187]

Executive Order 11491

In 1969, President Richard Nixon issued Executive Order 11491, which further developed the framework of federal labor-management relations. It provided that majority exclusive recognition would be the only form of union recognition,[188] established the Federal Labor Relations Council (the predecessor to the current Federal Labor Relations Authority, FLRA) and the Federal Service Impasses Panel (FSIP), and listed prohibited unfair labor practices for both unions and management. It also allowed employees to use limited "official time" to negotiate a collective bargaining agreement.[189]

The Federal Service Labor-Management Relations Statute

Although federal employees were given collective bargaining rights under the executive orders (EOs) issued by Presidents Kennedy and Nixon, those rights were not necessarily secure, as EOs are subject to unilateral change or termination by the President. In 1978, however, Congress codified and adopted many of the EOs' provisions as Title VII of the Civil Service Reform Act of 1978, commonly referred to as the Federal Service Labor-Management

Relations Statute (FSLMRS). While the statute followed the general principles of the EOs, it also made several changes, such as establishing the Federal Labor Relations Authority (FLRA), limiting the statute's coverage, and allowing employees official time to negotiate collective bargaining agreements.[190]

Recent Developments

In 2009, President Barack Obama issued Executive Order 13522, which created the National Council on Federal Labor-Management Relations (the Council). In this EO, the Council was charged with creating pilot labor-management forums within the federal government to allow agency managers and unions to discuss labor-management issues in a nonadversarial setting. The pilot project is in its third year and continues to implement new initiatives and advise the President on how to improve labor-management relations in the federal government.[191]

Other Federal Workforce Labor-Relations Statutes and Policies

Although several agencies were explicitly excluded from FSLMRS coverage (see "Employer Defined" below), some of them are covered by separate labor-relations statutes or policies.

The Government Accountability Office (GAO) is excluded from FSLMRS coverage, but the General Accounting Office Personnel Act of 1980 gave GAO employees the right to organize and bargain collectively.[192]

Neither the FSLMRS nor the Tennessee Valley Authority (TVA) Act of 1933 granted TVA employees collective bargaining rights. However, in 1935, TVA adopted a policy that allows employees to organize and bargain over wages.[193]

Without actually changing the language of the National Labor Relations Act (NLRA), Congress incorporated most NLRA provisions into the Postal Reorganization Act of 1970. This action gave enforceable collective bargaining rights to U.S. postal workers.[194]

Overview

The FSLMRS seeks to prevent labor-management disputes that could burden or obstruct federal government operations. It grants certain rights to both workers and employers, seeks to prevent practices that could frustrate a peaceful worker-employer relationship, and provides mechanisms for workers and employers to resolve disputes.

To achieve these goals, the FSLMR regulates the labor-management relationship between workers and employers in most federal agencies. It provides parties with a standard process for choosing a union to act as an employee representative in the collective bargaining process and details which individuals can participate in the process. Once a union is selected, the FSLMR governs which subjects workers and unions can negotiate. The FSMLRS also regulates how workers, employers, and unions should behave towards each other during the union selection and collective bargaining processes and prohibits certain unfair actions.

To administer and enforce the statute, the FSLMRS established the Federal Labor Relations Authority (FLRA) as the primary agency to administer and enforce the statute. The FLRA has the authority to investigate and adjudicate representation disputes, ULP complaints, and contract disputes. The Federal Mediation and Conciliation Service (FMCS) is an independent agency that provides voluntary mediation services to parties who cannot resolve a bargaining dispute. The Federal Service Impasses Panel (FSIP) is an entity within the FLRA that provides additional assistance in resolving disputes if FMCS services cannot resolve the dispute or if the parties specifically request FSIP's services.

Scope of Coverage

The FSLMRS regulates collective bargaining rights and duties for most federal agencies, employees, and unions. The preliminary sections of the FSLMRS define "employer," "employee," and "labor organization," and those definitions determine who is covered by the statute's regulations.

State and local laws govern state and local public employees.

Employer Defined

The FSLMRS applies to most federal executive agencies, along with the Library of Congress, the Government Printing Office, and the Smithsonian Institution. Several agencies are specifically excluded from the statute's coverage. Those excluded agencies are the Government Accountability Office, the Federal Bureau of Investigation, the Central Intelligence Agency, the National Security Agency, the Tennessee Valley Authority, the Federal Labor

Relations Authority, the Federal Impasses Panel, and the U.S. Secret Service.[195]

The President has the power to unilaterally exclude an agency or subdivision from coverage under the FSLMRS if he determines the entity's "primary function" is "intelligence, counterintelligence, investigative, or national security work" and that the provisions of the statute cannot be applied "in a manner consistent with national security requirements and considerations."[196] With this power, the President has excluded additional agencies and agency subdivisions, including the National Nuclear Security Administration, the Federal Air Marshall Service, and several subdivisions of each branch of the military.[197]

Employee Defined

An employee includes any individual employed in an agency or an individual who is no longer employed at an agency because of unfair labor practices and who has not obtained regular and substantially similar employment elsewhere. The definition specifically excludes some individuals from the definition of employee, including noncitizens, members of the uniformed services, supervisors, management officials, officers or employees in the Foreign Service, and individuals who participate in a strike in violation of the statute.[198]

Labor Organization Defined

A labor organization is defined as an organization composed, at least in part, of employees who participate in and pay dues to that organization. The organization must have the purpose of dealing with an agency regarding conditions of employment and grievances. Organizations that deny membership on the basis of sex, color, race, creed, national origin, and other similar characteristics; advocate the overthrow of the U.S. government; are sponsored by an agency; or participate or assist in a strike are not labor organizations recognized under the statute.[199]

Rights and Duties under the Law

The statute both mandates and prohibits certain actions of all parties involved in a labor- management dispute. The statute grants employees the right to organize and collectively bargain and sets forth the procedures and standards to be applied in the selection of a union as an employee representative and the subsequent relations between the union and the employer.

Unions and agencies can bargain over working conditions but cannot bargain over those topics already governed by another law (i.e., rates of pay as determined by the General Schedule). Working conditions might include work hours and allocation of employee offices. Employees must share a "community of interest" to be recognized as an appropriate unit for union representation. The union selection process is more limited in the federal sector than in the private sector, as a union can only be certified as an employee representative through a secret ballot election and union-security agreements are illegal.

Certain conduct is prohibited in the employer-union relationship during union organization and collective bargaining. Employers and unions cannot interfere with employees' right to organize and select a union. Employers and unions are required to bargain with each other in good faith, and employers can only bargain with an employee-selected union. If a bargaining impasse is reached, federal employees are prohibited from participating in strikes, work stoppages, slowdowns, or picketing that interferes with agency operations.

Bargaining Subjects

The FSLMRS gives federal employees the right to collectively bargain over conditions of employment.[200] Conditions of employment include "personnel policies, practices, and matters ... affecting work conditions." An employee's right to participate in political activities, the classification of positions, and any matters covered by other federal statutes (e.g., wages)[201] are specifically excluded from this definition.[202]

Employees and their unions are also not allowed to bargain over the statutory rights of management that are set forth in the statute. These nonnegotiable managerial rights include the authority to determine the organization's mission or budget and the authority to hire, discharge, or assign work to an employee.[203] The parties may, however, bargain over grievance procedures for adversely affected employees, the way in which management will exercise its authority, and, at the agency's election, the number of employees or positions assigned to a work project,[204]

Union Selection

Federal employees have the right to select their union, and agencies must give exclusive recognition to the union selected by employees.[205]

Union Security Agreements

Union security agreements are prohibited under the FSLMRS. Unions representing federal employees must represent all unit employees, regardless of whether they pay dues.[206]

Determination of a Bargaining Unit

Unions can represent those employees who are grouped together in an appropriate unit. To find a unit "appropriate" for representation, the FSLMRS requires that three criteria be met.

1. The unit must encompass employees who share a clear "community of interest," identifiable employment concerns distinct from those of other groups of employees.[207]
2. The unit must promote an effective relationship with the agency.
3. The unit must promote efficient operations of the agency.[208]

Management officials and supervisors cannot be included in a bargaining unit unless they have historically been included in the unit.[209] Additional employees prohibited from a unit include employees who administer FSLMRS provisions and employees whose work affects national security.[210]

Eligibility to Vote

The Federal Labor Relations Authority (FLRA) determines which employees are eligible to vote in secret ballot elections.[211] Regularly scheduled intermittent employees who work in positions that exist year round or who have a reasonable expectation of continued employment can vote in elections.[212] Temporary employees can also vote, if they have a reasonable expectation of continued employment beyond their initial six months of work and share a community of interest with the permanent employees included in the bargaining unit.[213]

Certification

Under the FSLMRS, a union can only be certified as an employee representative through a secret ballot election. To initiate a secret ballot election, an individual, a union, or an agency must first file a representation petition and a "showing of interest" that either 30% of unit employees wish to be represented by a union or that 30% of unit employees allege that the union no longer represents a majority of the unit employees.[214]

The regional director of the FLRA's General Counsel (see discussion of "FLRA Enforcement and Adjudication Processes" below) will determine whether the showing of interest is sufficient and meet with parties to resolve any preliminary disputes. It then conducts an investigation into any allegations made, including identifying related cases, identifying other parties who may be affected, and making any other necessary determinations.[215]

After an investigation and any hearings, the regional director can order a secret ballot election. If an election is ordered, parties are encouraged to enter into consent-election agreements that include the choices to be on the ballot and the method of election. However, if parties cannot agree to these terms, the regional director will issue a "direction of election." A direction of election sets out the election procedures. Parties have the opportunity to bring any nonprocedural issues before the regional director in a hearing.[216]

Once an election is held, a union will be certified as an employee representative if it receives the majority of votes cast. If an election has more than one union on the ballot and no choice receives a majority of the votes, the two choices with the most votes face each other in a runoff election.[217]

A party can file an objection to procedural aspects of an election or conduct that may have adversely impacted the election within five days of the vote tally.[218] While the results of an election are pending, parties must maintain the terms of any existing collective bargaining agreement.[219]

National Consultation Rights

The FSLMRS gives employees who are unrepresented by a certified union an additional collective bargaining protection. National Consultation Rights (NCRs)[220] entitle a union to be informed of agency-proposed substantive changes in employment conditions and to present its views and recommendations on the matter, even if the union does not have exclusive agency recognition. An agency must consider any views and recommendations submitted to it by a union with NCRs before making a final decision. A union gains NCRs if a unit does not have a recognized exclusive representative within its agency and the union is the exclusive representative of at least 3,500 or 10% of employees in the agency.[221]

Decertification

An election can also be held to determine if a bargaining unit no longer wishes to be represented by its union. As with a petition for a representation election, an individual, union, or agency can file a petition for an election, and the petition must be signed by or accompanied by authorization cards of 30% of the unit employees who allege that the union no longer represents a majority of the unit employees.[222]

Additionally, a regional director can revoke certification if a union disclaims its interest in representing the unit or if the regional director determines that the unit is no longer appropriate because of a "substantial change in character and scope of the unit" and that an election is unnecessary.[223]

Prohibited Conduct

The FSLMRS defines and prohibits certain conduct as unfair labor practices (ULPs) to protect the rights of both workers and employers.[224] The FLRA can issue cease-and-desist orders to stop a ULP, require employers to reinstate and give backpay to employees who were improperly discharged for union activities, and require parties to renegotiate contracts in accordance with its orders. A union may be required to give an employee backpay if it caused an employer to discharge that employee.[225]

During Union Organization Efforts

The FSLMRS protects employees' right to organize and imposes restrictions on employers and unions during this process. The statute prohibits employers and unions from interfering with or coercing employees exercising their right to organize. For instance, neither an employer nor a union can threaten discharge or make threatening statements to employees to influence their decision to join a union. A union cannot cause an employer to discriminate against employees regarding employment conditions.[226]

Agencies are prohibited from sponsoring, controlling, or assisting a union. Prohibited conduct includes actively assisting a union in organizing its employees or campaigning for a particular union or individual running for union office.[227]

During an Ongoing Employer-Union Relationship

Both employers and unions are required to negotiate in good faith with one another over conditions of employment. This obligation to negotiate includes, if requested by either party, the duty to enter into a written collective bargaining agreement. This obligation does not require either party to make a concession or agree to a proposal by the other party.[228]

The duty to bargain in good faith includes coming to the bargaining table with a willingness to reach a collective bargaining agreement and meeting at reasonable times and places. For instance, both employers and unions are required to bargain on negotiable matters proposed by the other that are not already in the collective bargaining agreement. Additionally, employers cannot unilaterally change working conditions. Working conditions might include work hours or allocation of employee offices. Neither employers nor unions can refuse to cooperate in impasse procedures and decisions. Failure to cooperate includes failing to comply with a final order from the Federal Service Impasses Panel, the FLRA's dispute resolution entity.[229]

Employers cannot discipline or discriminate against employees who file complaints under the statute. A union cannot coerce, discipline, fine, or attempt to coerce a union member as punishment or to hinder their work. Employees are protected from union harassment when they are performing their official work duties.[230] Additionally, unions cannot discriminate against employees regarding union membership because of race, color, creed, national origin, sex, age, civil service status, political affiliation, marital status, or handicap.[231] Neither employers nor unions can refuse to comply with any other provision of the statute.[232]

During Self-Help

Federal employees can use self-help to exert pressure on an employer, but the types of self-help available are more limited than under other labor relations laws. Federal employees can engage in peaceful, informational picketing so long as the activity does not interfere with agency operations. However, unlike private-sector employees, federal employees cannot participate in, and unions cannot encourage, strikes, work stoppages, slowdowns, or pickets that interfere with agency operations. Additionally, a union commits a ULP if it fails to prevent such activity. If a union willfully or intentionally supports such actions, the FLRA can revoke its exclusive recognition status.[233]

FSLMRS Enforcement and Adjudication Processes

The FSLMRS established the Federal Labor Relations Authority (FLRA) as the primary agency to administer and enforce the statute. The FLRA has the authority to investigate and adjudicate representation disputes, ULP complaints, and contract disputes. The Federal Mediation and Conciliation Service (FMCS) provides voluntary mediation services to parties who have reached a negotiation impasse. The Federal Service Impasses Panel (FSIP) is an entity within the FLRA that provides additional assistance in resolving disputes if FMCS services cannot resolve the dispute or if the parties specifically request FSIP's services. The FLRA's General Counsel investigates and prosecutes ULP complaints. FLRA decisions can be reviewed by federal courts in limited circumstances; judicial review of FSIP decisions is unavailable.

The Federal Labor Relations Authority

The FLRA is an independent federal agency charged with administering and enforcing the FSLMRS. It is composed of three members (the Authority) who are appointed by the President for five-year terms. No more than two can be of the same political party. Hereafter, "FLRA" refers to the three-member board, the General Counsel, and the FSIP as a collective body. The "Authority" refers to the three-member board alone. The Authority's responsibilities include hearing ULP cases, determining the appropriateness of units, and conducting secret ballot elections.[234]

The FLRA's General Counsel investigates and prosecutes complaints before the Authority and is appointed by the President for a five-year term. The FLRA can delegate its power to determine election issues and to investigate and prosecute ULP complaints to its seven regional offices.[235]

The Federal Mediation and Conciliation Service

FMCS provides mediation services for parties who have reached an impasse in negotiations. FMCS services are available to both private and public workers and employers. In the federal sector, use of FMCS services is voluntary. If federal parties are unable to resolve their dispute using FMCS services, they can request that FSIP consider the matter or they can agree to binding arbitration procedures. The arbitration procedures must be approved by FSIP.[236] To aid in arbitration, the FMCS maintains a list of approximately 1,400 independent arbitrators who can hear and decide disputes over collective bargaining interpretation or application.[237]

The Federal Service Impasses Panel

FSIP is an entity within the FLRA and provides assistance in resolving disputes between agencies and unions over working conditions.[238] FSIP comprises seven members who are appointed by the President and serve staggered five-year terms.[239]

If parties cannot resolve an impasse by using a third-party mediator or if either party requests FSIP's services, FSIP can make recommendations to the parties and assist them in resolving the dispute. If the parties still cannot come to an agreement, FSIP can impose an agreement on the parties.[240]

Judicial Review

Issues delegated to a regional director or administrative law judge can be reviewed and then affirmed, reversed, or modified by the Authority. In some cases, a party can also seek court review of a final order made by the Authority.[241] For a court to review a decision, generally, the Authority's determinations must be arbitrary or contrary to the law.[242] Direct judicial review of FSIP orders is unavailable.[243]

Dispute Resolution

Unfair Labor Practice Disputes

An employee, union, or agency can initiate a ULP investigation by filing a charge with an FLRA regional director. Generally, a charge must be filed no more than six months after the alleged ULP occurred. The charge is investigated by regional office staff, and the regional director, in his discretion, may issue a complaint, which sets forth the alleged ULP and the hearing date before an ALJ. If the regional director decides not to issue a complaint, the decision can be appealed to the General Counsel.[244]

Throughout the processing of a charge, the Authority offers parties voluntary alternative dispute resolution services, including training, education, and intervention at its Collaboration and Alternative Dispute Resolution Office (CADRO).[245]

If the regional director decides to issue a complaint and the parties are still unable to settle the dispute, the General Counsel prosecutes the complaint before an ALJ. The ALJ's decision can be reviewed by the Authority. If the Authority does not review the decision, the decision becomes the Authority's decision.[246]

If the Authority finds that a ULP has occurred, it can order an agency to reinstate an employee with backpay, the parties to enter into a collective bargaining agreement, a party to stop committing the ULP (cease-and-desist order), or any other action that would carry out the purpose of the statute.[247] Additionally, district courts can issue temporary relief (e.g., cease-and-desist orders) during the processing of a complaint if the General Counsel believes that not maintaining the status quo would frustrate the intent of the statute.[248]

Contract Disputes

Negotiability

Disputes over whether parties have an obligation to negotiate over a specific contract term generally fall into one of two categories: negotiability disputes and bargaining obligation disputes.

In a negotiability dispute, the agency and union disagree about whether a proposed contract term is contrary to the law such that the agency is not required to negotiate over it. If the agency contends it is not required to negotiate over a matter, the union may initiate a negotiability appeal in which it asks the Authority to review the matter.[249]

In a bargaining obligation dispute, an agency usually argues that it has no obligation to bargain over a matter because the proposal is already covered by an existing collective bargaining agreement, the union has waived the right to bargain, a change initiated by the agency is too minor to warrant bargaining, or the matter does not cover a condition of employment.

These disputes can be resolved through ULP resolution procedures, negotiated grievance procedures, or negotiability appeal procedures.[250]

To initiate procedures in a negotiability appeal, the union must file a petition with the Authority's Office of Case Control, not the regional office. The parties then explain their dispute to the Authority in a conference and a series of written allegations, and the Authority makes a decision. If at any time during the appeal, the parties express an interest in mediation, they will be referred to CADRO.[251]

Negotiated Grievance Procedures

All collective bargaining agreements are required to contain negotiated grievance procedures, which lay out procedures for settling grievances. These procedures must provide for binding arbitration if a grievance cannot be settled by the parties.

Usually, the procedures set forth in negotiated grievance procedures are the only procedures available for resolving grievances.[252]

A negotiated grievance procedure automatically covers all issues, except those excluded by law or those that parties explicitly exclude. Those subjects that are excluded from negotiated grievance procedures by the FSLMRS include retirement, life insurance, or health insurance benefits and suspension or removal for reasons of national security.

Procedures other than the negotiated grievance procedures exist for disputes involving a removal or demotion for unacceptable performance;

serious adverse actions, such as a reduction in grade or pay; employment discrimination allegations; personnel actions prohibited by statute; and unfair labor practices.[253]

Either party can file an exception to most arbitration awards with the Authority within 30 days of the award being served on the parties.[254] The Authority can make recommendations and take appropriate action regarding the award if it finds the award is contrary to law or on "other grounds similar to those applied by Federal courts in private sector labor-management relations."[255]

Impasses

Parties have several dispute resolution options when they have reached an impasse in the collective bargaining process. The agency and union may agree on a method to help resolve the dispute, such as binding private arbitration.[256] Parties can also voluntarily go to the FMCS for assistance to resolve an impasse.[257]

If parties have exhausted voluntary attempts to settle an impasse, either party can request that FSIP consider the issue. If FSIP asserts jurisdiction, it can either recommend dispute resolution procedures to the parties (e.g., refer the parties to CADRO) or assist them in resolving the impasse.

FSIP's procedures are generally informal, but it can hold hearings, administer oaths, issue subpoenas, and take any other necessary actions to resolve the impasse. Afterwards, FSIP makes a final decision and order, which is binding on the parties for the term of their agreement.[258]

Emergency Actions

Unlike the RLA and FLRA, the FSLMRS does not have any emergency dispute resolution provisions.

APPENDIX A. GLOSSARY OF TERMS

Adjustment Board	An entity that provides dispute resolution services.
Agency Shop	A type of union-security through which employees who do not become union members pay a fee to the union for its services as a bargaining agent.

Arbitration	Dispute resolution procedure in which parties present their arguments to a neutral party (arbitrator) who determines what the resolution to an issue should be. In binding arbitration, the arbitrator's decision is imposed on both parties. In nonbinding arbitration, the parties may choose to accept or reject the arbitrator's decision.
Authorization Card	A form evidencing that an individual employee wishes to be represented by a union.
Bargaining Unit/ Craft/Class	A group of employees who are or wish to be represented by a union.
Certification	The determination of the administrator of a secret ballot election that the results are the voting employees' wishes. The union that receives the majority valid votes cast will be certified as the employee representative.
Closed Shop	A type of union security that makes membership in a particular union a precondition to employment. Closed shops are generally prohibited.
Collective Bargaining	The process of negotiation about working conditions between a union and an employer.
Consent-Election Agreement	An employer-union agreement that contains terms of a secret ballot election agreed on by the parties and can include the election's time and place, choices to be included on the ballot, and the method to determine voting eligibility.
Decertification	The process through which a union loses NLRB recognition as a bargaining unit's exclusive representative.
Economic Strike	An employee work stoppage for the purpose of obtaining economic concessions.
Injunction	A court order requiring or restraining specifics acts.
Intermittent Strike	A series of employee work stoppages for a short period of time, followed by resumptions of work.
Mediation	A dispute resolution procedure in which parties work with a neutral party (mediator) who helps the parties reach an agreement on their issues.

	Mediators do not have the authority to impose a settlement on the parties.
Partial Strike	An action in which employees remain on work premises and refuse to work overtime, engage in work slowdowns, or choose to do some tasks but not others.
Presidential Emergency Board	A special entity created by the President if he believes that a labor dispute will substantially affect the nation's commerce. It can investigate and issue reports to the President on the labor dispute at hand.
Right-to-Work Law	A law that prohibits or restricts union security agreements.
Secondary Activity	An employee action to exert pressure on an entity outside of a specific dispute.
Secondary Boycott	An union attempt to influence an employer by either appealing to consumers to discontinue the use or purchase of a business's products or services or attempting to dissuade employees from working for a particular employer.
Secret ballot election	An election in which a person's vote is secret. This is the primary way in which a union gains certification as an exclusive employee representative.
Selective Striking	An employee work stoppage against one or a small number of employers as a means to reach an agreement with all the employers concerned.
Self-Help	A way in which one party can exert pressure on the other party that occurs outside of the formal dispute resolution process.
Sit-Down Strike	An employee work stoppage in which employees take possession of the employer's property and exclude others from entering.
Status Quo	The rates of pay, rules, and work conditions in effect before a dispute arises.
Sympathy Strike	An employee work stoppage for the purpose of supporting a cause or another group of strikers.

Unfair Labor Practice	An action taken by an employer or a union that interferes with a party's rights under federal labor-management relations statutes.
Unfair Labor Practice Strike	An employee work stoppage for the purpose of protecting an unfair labor practice.
Union Security Agreement	An employer-union agreement that requires employees to pay union dues equal to the cost of representation as a condition of employment.
Union Shop	A type of union security that requires employees to become and remain a union member as a condition of employment after 30 days of employment. Union shops are generally legal.
Voluntary Recognition	An employer's choice to recognize a union as the exclusive employee representative without the use of a secret ballot election.

APPENDIX B. LIST OF ACRONYMS

ALJ	Administrative Law Judge
CADRO	Collaboration and Alternative Dispute Resolution Office
EO	Executive Order
FAA	Federal Aviation Administration
FLRA	Federal Labor Relations Authority
FMCS	Federal Mediation and Conciliation Service
FSIP	Federal Service Impasses Panel
FSLMRS	Federal Service Labor-Management Relations Statute
GAO	Government Accountability Office
NCR	National Consultation Right
NLRA	National Labor Relations Act
NLRB	National Labor Relations Board
NMB	National Mediation Board
NRAB	National Railroad Adjustment Board
PEB	Presidential Emergency Board
RLA	Railway Labor Act
SBA	Special Board of Adjustment
TVA	Tennessee Valley Authority
ULP	Unfair Labor Practice

Appendix C. Comparison of RLA, NLRA, and FSLMRA Key Provisions

Statutory Provision	RLA	NLRA	FSLMRS
Statute Citation	45 U.S.C. §151 et seq.	29 U.S.C. §141 et seq.	5 U.S.C. §7101 et seq.
Administrative Agency	• National Mediation Board • National Railroad Adjustment Board • System Boards of Adjustment	• National Labor Relations Board	• Federal Labor Relations Authority • Federal Mediation and Conciliation Service • Federal Service Impasses Panel
Coverage	Railway and airline carriers	Private employers, excluding railway and airline carriers	Federal agencies, excluding those specifically excepted
Union Selection	• Secret Ballot Election	• Secret Ballot Election	• Secret Ballot Election
	• Voluntary Recognition	• Voluntary Recognition • NLRB-Mandated Recognition	
Union Security Clauses	Allowed	Allowed, unless prohibited by state law	Prohibited
Bargaining Subjects	"Rates of pay, rules, and working conditions"	"Rates of pay, wages, hours of employment, and other conditions of employment"	"Personnel policies, practices, and matters" not otherwise provided for by statute or relating to position classification
Unfair Labor Practices	General rules of fair dealing found in 45 U.S.C. §152.	Specific provisions found in 29 U.S.C. §158.	Specific provisions found in 5 U.S.C. §7116.
Dispute Resolution	Mediation and Arbitration	Voluntary settlement or formal adjudicatory proceedings	Voluntary dispute resolution services or formal adjudicatory proceedings
Self-Help	Most self-help is allowed, so long as it is not unlawful or "inherently destructive" of union or employer activity. Some allowed activities are intermittent and selective striking and secondary activity.	Self-help is allowed, so long as it is not violent, unlawful, or unjustifiably injurious to employer interests. Some prohibited activities include intermittent and partial strikes, acts of disloyalty, and some secondary activities.	Limited forms of self-help are allowed, including informational picketing. Prohibited self-help includes strikes, work stoppages, slowdowns, and pickets that interfere with agency operations.
Emergency Procedures	Presidential emergency board with potential congressional action	Presidential "board of inquiry" with potential congressional action	None

Source: CRS analysis.

End Notes

[1] Rudolph Daniels, *Trains Across the Continent: North America Railroad History*, 2nd ed. (Bloomington: Indiana University Press, 2000), p. 49.
[2] Frank N. Wilner, *The Railway Labor Act and the Dilemma of Labor Relations* (Omaha: Simmons-Boardman Books, Inc., 1991), p. 25.
[3] The Brotherhood of Locomotive Engineers was the first railway union, organizing in 1863; the Order of the Railway Conductors, the Brotherhood of Locomotive Firemen, and the Brotherhood of Railroad Trainmen formed shortly thereafter. Ibid., p. 26.
[4] Previous legislative efforts to regulate labor relations include Arbitration Act of 1888, 25 Stat. 501 (1888); Erdman Act, 30 Stat. 424 (1898); Newlands Act 38 Stat. 103 (1913); Adamson Act 39 Stat. 721 (1916); and Transportation Act of 1920, 41 Stat. 456 (1920). For an overview of this legislative history, see Wilner, *The Railway Labor Act & the Dilemma of Labor Relations*, pp. 29-49.
[5] Ibid., pp. 47-49.
[6] 45 U.S.C. §151a.
[7] American Bar Association, "Introduction," in *The Railway Labor Act*, ed. Douglas L. Leslie (Washington, D.C.: BNA Books, 1995), p. 47 (Hereafter cited as ABA, *The Railway Labor Act*).
[8] 45 U.S.C. §153, First (l).
[9] 45 U.S.C. §152, Third, Tenth.
[10] 45 U.S.C. §156.
[11] 45 U.S.C. §151, First.
[12] Most provisions of the RLA, 45 U.S.C. §§151-163, apply to air carriers. 45 U.S.C. §153, which establishes the National Railroad Adjustment Board, does not apply to air carriers. Title III of the RLA codifies the inclusion of air carriers under the RLA. The aviation manufacturing (defense, space, and commercial) and general aviation (e.g., flight training, intercontinental jet transportation of executives and public officers) industries fall under the NLRA's jurisdiction.
[13] U.S. Congress, Senate Committee on Interstate Commerce, *To Amend the Railway Labor Act to Cover Every Common Carrier by Air Engaged in Interstate or Foreign Commerce*, hearing on S. 2496, 74th Cong., 2nd sess., May 20, 1935, pp. 4-10. Carriers neither supported nor actively opposed the legislation. ABA, "Introduction," in *The Railway Labor Act*, p. 56.
[14] 45 U.S.C. §152, Eleventh.
[15] 45 U.S.C. §153, Second. Jacob Seidenberg, "Grievance Adjustment in the Railroad Industry," in *The Railway Labor Act at Fifty: Collective Bargaining in the Railroad and Airline Industries*, ed. Charles M. Rehmus (Washington, D.C.: National Mediation Board, 1977), pp. 223-224.
[16] 45 U.S.C. 159a (c).
[17] 29 C.F.R. §1206.2. Larry Swisher, "NMB Ends Longstanding Policy, Adopts Rule for Majority Vote in Representation Elections," *Daily Labor Report*, May 11, 2010, p. AA-1.
[18] 29 C.F.R §1206.1(b).
[19] *FAA Modernization and Reform Act of 2012*, P.L. 112-95 (2012).
[20] Ibid.
[21] 45 U.S.C. §151, First.
[22] 45 U.S.C. §151.
[23] 45 U.S.C. §151, Fifth.
[24] National Mediation Board, *Representation Manual*, March 21, 2011, §9.2, http://www.nmb.gov/representation/representation-manual.pdf (hereafter cited as NMB, *Representation Manual*).
[25] 45 U.S.C. §152, Third, Fourth.
[26] 45 U.S.C. §152, Ninth.

[27] NMB, *Representation Manual*, §9.1.

[28] The following is a list of some of the well-recognized traditional crafts or classes: Locomotive Engineers; Locomotive Firemen and Hostlers; Conductors; Trainmen; Yardmen; Yardmasters; Office, Station, and Store Employees; Telegraph Workers; Dispatchers; Signalmen; Maintenance of Way Employees; Machinists; Boilermakers and Blacksmiths; Sheet Metal Workers; Electrical Workers; Dining Car Attendants; Carmen and Coach Cleaners; and Powerhouse Employees and Shop Laborers. ABA, "Selecting A Bargaining Representative," in *The Railway Labor Act*, pp. 98-99.

[29] Some of the traditional crafts or classes within the airline industry include ground personnel (mechanics, ground service personnel, and plant maintenance personnel), clerical and office employees, fleet and passenger service employees, deck crew, and cabin crew. ABA, "Selecting A Bargaining Representative," in *The Railway Labor Act*, pp. 100-105.

[30] National Mediation Board, *Annual Performance and Accountability Report FY2011*, November 14, 2011, p. 27, http://www.nmb.gov/documents/2011annual-report/pdf/NMB2011_00_full.pdf (hereafter cited as NMB, FY2011).

[31] An individual must be employed in the craft on and after the cut-off date. The cut-off date is the last day of the payroll period ending before an application was submitted to the NMB.

[32] NMB, *Representation Manual*, §9.2.

[33] 45 U.S.C. §152, Ninth.

[34] 45 U.S.C. §152, Twelfth. The NMB can dismiss applications for investigation under one of several election bar doctrines. Under these doctrines, the NMB, generally, will dismiss an application for a specific amount of time after an election has been held or a previous application has been filed between the same craft and carrier as in the current election or application before it. 29 C.F.R. §1206.4.

[35] NMB, *Representation Manual*, §§2.0-5.0.

[36] 29 C.F.R. §1202.4. Bureau of National Affairs, "NMB Ends Longstanding Policy, Adopts Rule For Majority Vote in Representation Elections," *Daily Labor Report*, no. 89, May 11, 2010, p. AA-1.

[37] *FAA Modernization and Reform Act of 2012*, Public Law No: 112-95 (2012).

[38] NMB, *Representation Manual*, §7.0.

[39] ABA, "Selecting a Bargaining Representative," in *The Railway Labor Act*, p. 107.

[40] ABA, "Selecting a Bargaining Representative," in *Railway Labor Act*, pp. 135-137.

[41] See 45 U.S.C. §152, Fourth.

[42] 45 U.S.C. §152, First.

[43] William E. Thoms and Frank J. Dooley, "Collective Bargaining Under the Railway Labor Act," *Transportation Law Journal*, vol. 20 (1991), p. 280.

[44] 45 U.S.C. §152, Third. Instances of carrier interference include firing or demoting employees for supporting a union, giving employees inaccurate information about an election, favoring one union candidate over another, granting or withholding benefits, and making threats. ABA, "Protection of Employees' Right of Self-Organization," in *The Railway Labor Act*, pp. 163-173.

[45] 45 U.S.C. §152, Fourth.

[46] 45 U.S.C. §152, Fifth.

[47] 45 U.S.C. §152, Tenth.

[48] 45 U.S.C. §152, Ninth.

[49] Ibid.

[50] ABA, "Protection of Employees' Right to Self-Organization," in *The Railway Labor Act*, pp. 186-187, 200-202.

[51] For instance, a union may appeal to consumers to discontinue use or purchase of a business's products or services or attempt to dissuade employees from working for a particular employer.

[52] ABA, "Exercise of Economic Weapons," in *The Railway Labor Act*, pp. 320-321.

[53] ABA, "Negotiation of Collective Bargaining Agreements," in *The Railway Labor Act*, pp. 241-242.
[54] 45 U.S.C. §154, First.
[55] See NMB, *FY2011*, pp. 4, 8.
[56] 45 U.S.C. §153, First, (a).
[57] The NRAB's First Division processes disputes involving "operating" employees (e.g., engineers). The Second Division processes disputes involving "shop" employees (e.g., repairmen). The Third Division processes dispute involving employees in miscellany crafts, and the Fourth Division processes disputes involving employees who transport passengers or property by water. 45 U.S.C. §153, First, (h).
[58] 45 U.S.C. §153, First, (p) and (q).
[59] 45 U.S.C. §153, Second.
[60] NMB, *FY2011*, p. 21. The daily pay rate for arbitrators on the NMB's Roster of Arbitrators is $300 per day. National Mediation Board, *Frequently Asked Questions: Arbitration*, http://www.nmb.gov/arbitration
[61] 45 U.S.C. §185.
[62] 45 U.S.C. §184.
[63] NMB, *FY2011*, p. 21.
[64] 45 U.S.C. §159.
[65] 45 U.S.C. §153, First (p) & (q).
[66] 45 U.S.C. §159, Second.
[67] ABA, "Enforcement of Collective Bargaining Agreements," in *The Railway Labor Act*, p. 269.
[68] See 45 U.S.C. §152, Ninth.
[69] ABA, "Negotiation of Collective Bargaining Agreements," in *The Railway Labor Act*, p. 251.
[70] 45 U.S.C. §156. "Status quo" refers to the rates of pay, rules, and work conditions in effect before a dispute arises. The purpose of maintaining the status quo during a dispute is to prevent either party from engaging in self-help until all negotiation and mediation procedures have been exhausted. ABA, "Negotiation of Collective Bargaining Agreements," in *The Railway Labor Act*, p. 232.
[71] 45 U.S.C. §155.
[72] ABA, "Selecting a Bargaining Representative," in *The Railway Labor Act*, pp. 128-129.
[73] 45 U.S.C. §155, First.
[74] 45 U.S.C. §156.
[75] 45 U.S.C. §157, First. The parties can also choose a six-member arbitration board where each party selects two members of the board; those four members, by a majority vote, then select two other arbitrators. If they fail to select the remaining two arbitrators, the NMB will select them.
[76] 45 U.S.C. §159, Second.
[77] 45 U.S.C. §152.
[78] ABA, "Negotiation of Collective Bargaining Agreements," in *The Railway Labor Act*, p. 234. Although carriers are not required to maintain the status quo in minor disputes, injunctions may be issued to preserve the status quo until the dispute is resolved. The Norris-LaGuardia Act, which generally prohibits courts from issuing injunctions in labor disputes, does not apply to disputes under the RLA. Injunctions are allowed against parties who violate the status quo provisions of the RLA. See ABA, "Enforcement of Collective Bargaining Agreements," in *The Railway Labor Act*, pp. 290-295.
[79] 45 U.S.C. §153, First, (j) and (o).
[80] 45 U.S.C. §153, Second.
[81] Ibid.
[82] 45 U.S.C. §160.
[83] 45 U.S.C. §159a.
[84] ABA, "Negotiation of Collective Bargaining Agreements," in *The Railway Labor Act*, p. 221. For example, in P.L. 88-108, Congress established an arbitration board to resolve a dispute

over the use of railroad firemen and manning levels for railroad crews. Congress has also created its own compromise packages and imposed settlements from other disputes on uncompromising unions. William E. Thoms and Frank J. Dooley, "Collective Bargaining Under the Railway Labor Act," *Transportation Law Journal*, vol. 20 (1991), pp. 224, 279.

[85] Benjamin J. Taylor and Fred Whitney, *U.S. Labor Relations Law: Historical Development* (Englewood Cliffs, NJ: Prentice Hall, 1992), pp. 153-154 (hereafter cited as Taylor & Whitney, *U.S. Labor Relations Law*).

[86] NIRA also did not provide enforcement procedures, specify prohibited antiunion conduct, require employers to bargain with employee-chosen representatives, or prohibit employer discrimination against employees for union activities. Ibid., pp. 154-155.

[87] Richard D. Polenberg, *The Era of Franklin D. Roosevelt 1933-1945* (Boston: Bedford/St. Martin's, 2000), pp. 68-69. For a statistical assessment of union growth after the NLRA was enacted, see Taylor & Whitney, *U.S. Labor Relations Law*, pp. 198-200.

[88] For instance, under the NLRA as originally enacted, no remedy existed against unions who imposed their will on employees, therefore, some unions used intimidation to garner support, rather than campaign for votes. Gerard D. Reilly, "The Legislative History of the Taft-Hartley Act," *George Washington Law Review*, vol. 29 (1960), pp. 286-287.

[89] 29 U.S.C. §158.

[90] 29 U.S.C. §158(a)(1) & (b)(1)(A). A closed shop is one in which an employer is required to employ only members of a particular union. Employers may hire anyone, but that person will be required to join the union within a specified amount of time. While these are prohibited under the NLRA, they are permitted under the Railway Labor Act. See "Railway Labor Act: Union Security Agreements," *supra*.

[91] 29 U.S.C. §158 (b)(3)(A).

[92] 29 U.S.C. §159(c)(1)(B).

[93] 29 U.S.C. §152.

[94] 29 U.S.C. §159(c)(1)(A).

[95] 29 U.S.C. §153.

[96] In the statute's declaration of findings, purposes, and policies, Congress stated:

> [T]here have been a number of instances of breach of trust, corruption, disregard of the rights of individual employees, and other failures to observe high standards of responsibility and ethical conduct which require further and supplementary legislation that will afford necessary protection of the rights and interests of employees and the public generally as they relate to the activities of labor organizations, employers, labor relations consultants, and their officers and representatives. (29 U.S.C. §401(b))

[97] 29 U.S.C. §§411, 431.

[98] 29 U.S.C. §481.

[99] Robert W. Kaps, *Air Transport Labor Relations* (Southern Illinois University Press, 1997), pp. 5-9.

[100] 29 U.S.C. §152.

[101] NLRB, *Basic Guide to the NLRA*, pp. 33-34, https://www.nlrb.gov/sites/default/files/documents/224/basicguide.pdf. CRS Report RL32930, *Labor Union Certification Procedures: Use of Secret Ballots and Card Checks*, by Gerald Mayer.

[102] 29 U.S.C. §152(2).

[103] ABA, "Jurisdiction: Coverage of the Act," in *The Developing Labor Law*, vol. 2, p. 2253.

[104] 29 U.S.C. §152(3). The Re-empowerment of Skilled and Professional Employees and Construction Tradeworkers (RESPECT) Act, S. 2168, was introduced in March, 2012. This amendment to the NLRB sought to narrow the definition of "supervisor," allowing employees who spend small amounts of time performing supervisory functions to participate in union activities.

[105] The NLRB reasons that the relationship between a university and a graduate student is primarily an educational one, such that graduate students who are also teaching assistants

are not covered by the NLRA. *Brown University and International Union*, 432 NLRB, pp. 488-489 (2004).

[106] 29 U.S.C. §152(11).

[107] ABA, "Jurisdiction: Coverage of the Act," in *The Developing Labor Law*, vol. 2, pp. 2271-2272.

[108] *General Dynamics Corp., Convair Aerospace Division and National Engineers and Professionals Association*, 213 NLRB 857 (1974).

[109] 29 U.S.C. §157.

[110] 29 U.S.C. §159(a).

[111] CRS Report RL32930, *Labor Union Certification Procedures: Use of Secret Ballots and Card Checks*, by Gerald Mayer.

[112] 29 U.S.C. §158(a)(3).

[113] 29 U.S.C. §158(e).

[114] 29 U.S.C. §164(b). For additional information on right-to-work laws, see CRS Report R42575, *Right to Work Laws: Legislative Background and Empirical Research*, by Benjamin Collins.

[115] ABA, "Union Security," in *The Developing Labor Law*, pp. 2149-2150. The construction industry standards for union security agreements are covered by a separate section of the act, 29 U.S.C. §158(f), because of the irregular nature of construction employment.

[116] CRS Report RL32930, *Labor Union Certification Procedures: Use of Secret Ballots and Card Checks*, by Gerald Mayer. NLRB, *Basic Guide to the NLRA*, pp. 12-13. The NLRB recently issued a new rule to expedite pre-election proceedings. 29 C.F.R. §102.64. The new rule went into effect April 30, 2012. In May 2012, the NLRB announced it would temporarily suspend this new rule in response to a U.S. District Court decision that found that, at the time the final rule was issued, the NLRB did not have the required quorum to issue the rule. National Labor Relations Board, "NLRB suspends implementation of representation case amendments based on court ruling," press release, May 15, 2012, http://www.nlrb.gov/news/nlrb-suspends-implementation-representation-case-amendments-based-court- ruling. Additionally, Members of both houses filed joint resolutions "disapproving" of the rule, stating that expedited pre-election procedures would deprive workers of sufficient time to make important decisions about union representation. Lawrence E. Dubé, "Legislators File Senate, House Resolutions," *Daily Labor Report*, February 16, 2012, p. A-17.

[117] An economic strike is one for the purpose of obtaining economic concessions, like higher wages.

[118] NLRB, *Basic Guide to the NLRA*, p. 16.

[119] ABA, "The Primary Strike," in *The Developing Labor Law*, p. 1597.

[120] 29 U.S.C. §159.

[121] NLRB, *Basic Guide to the NLRA*, p. 16.

[122] See 29 C.F.R. §101.19. NLRB, *Basic Guide to the NLRA*, p. 16.

[123] 29 C.F.R. §101.19.

[124] CRS Report RL32930, *Labor Union Certification Procedures: Use of Secret Ballots and Card Checks*, by Gerald Mayer. NLRB, *Basic Guide to the NLRA*, p. 16.

[125] 29 C.F.R. §§102.66-102.67.

[126] 29 U.S.C. §159.

[127] NLRB, *Basic Guide to the NLRA*, pp. 16-17.

[128] CRS Report RL32930, *Labor Union Certification Procedures: Use of Secret Ballots and Card Checks*, by Gerald Mayer. NLRB, *Basic Guide to the NLRA*, p. 16.

[129] CRS Report RL32930, *Labor Union Certification Procedures: Use of Secret Ballots and Card Checks*, by Gerald Mayer.

[130] The "reasonable amount of time" rule was the long-held NLRB rule until 2007 when the NLRB decided that employees could file a petition within 45 days of recognition. In August, 2011, the NLRB revised its position, stating that it was wholly unsupported by any

empirical evidence. The NLRB will look to several factors in determining a reasonable amount of time, including progress made in the negotiation process, whether the parties are negotiating an initial contract, and whether the parties are at an impasse. *Lamons Gasket Company and United Steel, Paper and Forestry, Rubber, Manufacturing, and Energy, Allied Industrial and Service Workers International Union*, 357 NLRB No. 72, p. 10 (2011), http://nlrb.gov/case/16-RD-001597.

[131] CRS Report RL32930, *Labor Union Certification Procedures: Use of Secret Ballots and Card Checks*, by Gerald Mayer.

[132] Ibid. NLRB, *Basic Guide to the NLRA*, p. 37.

[133] CRS Report RL32930, *Labor Union Certification Procedures: Use of Secret Ballots and Card Checks*, by Gerald Mayer. NLRB, *Basic Guide to the NLRA*, p. 14.

[134] CRS Report RL32930, *Labor Union Certification Procedures: Use of Secret Ballots and Card Checks*, by Gerald Mayer.

[135] 29 U.S.C. §159(a).

[136] ABA, "Subjects of Bargaining," in *The Developing Labor Law*, vol. 1, pp. 1247, 1263.

[137] Ibid., pp. 1264-1299.

[138] Ibid., pp. 1362-1386.

[139] The Taft-Hartley Act prohibited closed shops. Hot-cargo clauses are those in which the employer agrees to stop handling, using, or selling products of another employer. 29 U.S.C. §158(e).

[140] ABA, "Subjects of Bargaining," in *The Developing Labor Law*, vol. 1, pp. 1393-1397.

[141] 29 U.S.C. §158. 29 U.S.C. §160(c).

[142] 29 U.S.C. §160(c). NLRB, *Basic Guide to the NLRA*, p. 35, 38.

[143] 29 U.S.C. §160(c). NLRB, *Basic Guide to the NLRA*, p. 38. The amount of back pay awarded is the amount of compensation (i.e., wages plus benefits) that a worker would have received if he or she had not been unlawfully fired, less the amount of compensation received (less the expenses from looking for work) from other work during the back pay period, plus interest accrued. National Labor Relations Board, *NLRB Casehandling Manual, Part 3, Compliance Proceedings*, §10536, http://www.nlrb.gov/sites/default/files/documents/44/compliancemanual.pdf.

[144] 29 U.S.C. §§158(a)(1), (b)(1)(A).

[145] ABA, "Interference with Protected Rights," in *The Developing Labor Law*, vol. 1, p. 93.

[146] CRS Report RL32930, *Labor Union Certification Procedures: Use of Secret Ballots and Card Checks*, by Gerald Mayer.

[147] 29 U.S.C. §158(a)(2). NLRB, *Basic Guide to the NLRA*, p. 18.

[148] 29 U.S.C. §158(b)(1)(B).

[149] 29 U.S.C. §158(b)(1)(A).

[150] 29 U.S.C. §§158(a)(5), (b)(3), (d).

[151] ABA, "The Duty to Bargain," in *The Developing Labor Law*, vol. 1, pp. 827-846.

[152] 29 U.S.C. §§158(a)(1), (b)(1)(A).

[153] 29 U.S.C. §§158(a)(3), (a)(4).

[154] 29 U.S.C. §158(b)(2).

[155] ABA, "Interference with Protected Rights," in *The Developing Labor Law*, vol. 1, pp. 256-276.

[156] To be a "protected" activity, conduct must be for collective bargaining or for "mutual aid or protection" and concerted in nature. 29 U.S.C. §157.

[157] Acts of disloyalty include breach of confidentiality and false allegations about the employer.

[158] ABA, "Interference with Protected Rights," in *The Developing Labor Law*, vol. 1, pp. 196-254.

[159] NLRB, *Basic Guide to the NLRA*, p. 10.

[160] Serious misconduct includes violence and threats of violence and physically blocking individual from entering or leaving the workspace. Ibid., p. 11.

[161] Ibid., p. 10.

[162] ABA, "Interference with Protected Rights," in *The Developing Labor Law*, vol. 1, pp. 984-988.

[163] In January, 2012, President Barack Obama made three recess appointments to the NLRB during a three-day intra- session recess. Past Department of Justice (DOJ) briefs implied that the President may make a recess appointment during a recess lasting longer than three days. These appointments were considered by some to be controversial, because Congress had apparently scheduled its recesses to prevent recess appointments, but DOJ indicated that "the Administration does not regard congressional scheduling practices ... as an impediment to the exercise of the recess appointment power." CRS Report R42329, *Recess Appointments Made by President Barack Obama*, by Henry B. Hogue and Maureen Bearden. CRS Report RS21308, *Recess Appointments: Frequently Asked Questions*, by Henry B. Hogue.

[164] The Board has complete authority over all representation matters but has delegated much of this power to its regional directors. It still retains the power to review any regional director's decision. NLRB, *Basic Guide to the NLRA*, p. 7, 33. Feldacker, *Labor Guide to Labor Law*, pp. 39-44.

[165] NLRB, *Basic Guide the NLRA*, p. 33. Lawrence E. Dubé, "Obama Seeks 5 Percent NLRB Budget Rise," *Daily Labor Report*, February 13, 2012, p. C-2.

[166] 29 U.S.C. §160(f).

[167] The Board, not the parties, files a petition to enforce its order. 29 U.S.C. §160(e).

[168] For instance, a court set aside NLRB certification when it found that the NLRB had exceeded its statutory authority by certifying a union that included both professional and nonprofessional employees without giving the professional employees a separate election to determine whether they wished to be included in the unit. *Leedom v. Kyne*, 258 U.S. 184 (1958).

[169] ABA, "Judicial Review and Enforcement," in *The Developing Labor Law*, pp. 2803-2805.

[170] 29 U.S.C. §160(l).

[171] 29 U.S.C. §160(b).

[172] NLRB, *A Basic Guide the NLRA*, p. 36.

[173] ABA, "The NLRB Procedures," in *The Developing Labor Law*, vol. 2, pp. 2683-2688.

[174] Ibid., p. 2691.

[175] ABA, "NLRB Procedures," in *The Developing Labor Law*, vol. 2, pp. 2692-2701.

[176] 29 U.S.C. §185(a). ABA, "Board Action and Contract Enforcement," in *The Developing Labor Law*, vol. 1, pp. 1424-1427.

[177] The Taft-Hartley Act gave courts jurisdiction over contract disputes as a way to make collective bargaining agreements more readily enforceable. ABA, "Board Action and Contract Enforcement," in *The Developing Labor Law*, vol. 1, pp. 1408, 1476-1480.

[178] ABA, "Board Action and Contract Enforcement," in *The Developing Labor Law*, vol. 1, pp. 1435-1448.

[179] 29 U.S.C. §§176-177.

[180] 29 U.S.C. §178.

[181] 29 U.S.C. §179.

[182] 29 U.S.C. §180.

[183] By 1960, approximately 30% of nonagricultural private sector employees were represented by unions. Charles M. Rehmus, "Labor Relations in the Public Sector in the United States," *International Labour Review*, vol. 109, no. 3 (1974), p. 200. Although an estimated 30% of federal employees were represented by unions in 1961, most of those were U.S. Postal Service employees. The Government Printing Office and the Tennessee Valley Authority also held some collective bargaining rights, but most employees from other agencies did not. Approximately 16% of non-postal service federal employees were union members. See Kenneth Bullock, "Official Time as a Form of Union Security in Federal Sector Labor-Management Issues," *The Air Force Law Review*, vol. 59 (2007), pp. 164-167.

[184] Charles M. Rehmus, "Labor Relations in the Public Sector in the United States," *International Labour Review*, vol. 109, no. 3 (1974), pp. 201-202.

[185] Ibid., p. 202.

[186] Kenneth Bullock, "Official Time as a Form of Union Security in Federal Sector Labor-Management Issues," *The Air Force Law Review*, vol. 59 (2007), pp. 169-173.

[187] Executive Order 10988, "Employee-Management Cooperation in the Federal Service," *27 Federal Register* 551, January 17, 1962.

[188] Under majority exclusive recognition, once a union is recognized as the exclusive unit representative, an agency can collectively bargain with only that union.

[189] Executive Order 11491, "Labor-management relations in the Federal Service," 34 *Federal Register* 17,605, October 29, 1969.

[190] 5 U.S.C. §7131 (a). CRS Report R41732, *Collective Bargaining and Employees in the Public Sector*, by Jon O. Shimabukuro.

[191] Louis C. LaBrecque, "Obama Order Creates Federal Labor Council; No Mandate to Bargain on Permissive Topics," *Daily Labor Report*, December 12, 2009, p. A-14. For additional information on the National Council on Federal Labor-Management Relations, see its website, http://www.lmrcouncil.gov/index.aspx.

[192] P.L. 96-191. In 2007, analysts at GAO voted to be represented by the International Federation of Professional and Technical Engineers (IFPTE). In February 2012, support employees at GAO also voted to be represented by IFPTE.

[193] U.S. General Accounting Office, *Labor-Management Relations: Tennessee Valley Authority Situation Needs to Improve*, GAO/GGD-91-129, September 1991, http://archive.gao.gov/d18t9/145065.pdf.

[194] 39 U.S.C. §1201 et seq.

[195] 5 U.S.C. §7103(a)(3).

[196] 5 U.S.C. §7103(b)(1)(B).

[197] Executive Order 12171, "Exclusions from the Federal Labor-Management Relations Program," 3 C.F.R. §§1979 Comp., p. 458. Executive Order 13480, "Exclusions from the Federal Labor-Management Relations Program," 73 C.F.R. §234.

[198] 5 U.S.C. §1703(a)(2)(B). Although members of the uniformed services are broadly excluded from the statute's coverage, some members of the National Guard are protected under the statute. See, e.g., *Spence v. Holesinger*, 696 F. Supp. 398 (C.D. Ill. 1988).

[199] 5 U.S.C. §7103(a)(4).

[200] 5 U.S.C. §7101.

[201] 5 U.S.C. §5332. Employees at agencies excluded from the statute's coverage may be able to bargain over wages, depending on the statute that covers collective bargaining in their agency. See "Other Federal Workforce Labor- Relations Statutes and Policies," *supra*.

[202] 5 U.S.C. §7103(a)(14).

[203] 5 U.S.C. §7106(a).

[204] 5 U.S.C. §7106(b).

[205] 5 U.S.C. §7111.

[206] 5 U.S.C. §7114(a)(1).

[207] 5 U.S.C. §7112(a).

[208] Federal Labor Relations Authority, *A Guide to the Federal Service Labor-Management Relations Program* (2001), p. 6 (Hereafter cited as FLRA, *A Guide to the FLMRP*).

[209] A management official is an individual who has the duty or authority to determine or influence agency policy. 5 U.S.C. §7103(a)(11). A supervisor is an individual who has the authority to use independent judgment to take personnel actions, such as hiring, firing, or disciplining employees. 5 U.S.C. §7103(a)(10).

[210] FLRA, *A Guide to the FLMRP*, pp. 6-7.

[211] 5 U.S.C. §7111(d).

[212] See *Army & Air Force Exchange Service, Panama Area Exchange and ALF-CIO Local 907*, 7 F.L.R.A. 514 (1981). *For Buchanan Installation Club Management System and Congreso de Uniones Industriales de Puerto Rico*, 9 F.L.R.A. 143 (1982).

[213] See *Small Business Administration and AFGE*, 16 F.L.R.A. 180 (1984).

[214] 5 U.S.C. §7111 (b). The FLRA can dismiss applications for investigation under one of several election bar doctrines. Under these doctrines, the FLRA, generally, will dismiss an application for a specific amount of time after an election has been held or a previous application has been filed between the same bargaining unit and agency as in the current election or application before it. 5 C.F.R. §2422.12. Federal Labor Relations Authority Office of the General Counsel, *Representation Case Law Guide* (2000), pp. 128-129, http://www.flra.gov/webfm_send/27.

[215] If a party disputes the status of an organization as a "labor organization" under the statute, it can do so for one of two reasons. A party can either assert that the union does not fall within the definition of "labor organization" under the statute or that a union should not be given exclusive representative status when it is subject to corrupting influences. Federal Labor Relations Authority Office of General Counsel, *Representation Proceeding: Case Handling Manual* (2000), pp. 99-100, 263, 275-276, http://www.flra.gov/webfm_send/33.

[216] 5 C.F.R. §2422.16. FLRA, *A Guide to the FLMRP*, p. 13.

[217] 5 U.S.C. §7111.

[218] 5 C.F.R. §2422.26.

[219] 5 C.F.R. §2422.34.

[220] 5 U.S.C. §7113.

[221] Ibid. FLRA, *A Guide to the FLMRP*, p. 10.

[222] 5 U.S.C. §7111(b).

[223] 5 C.F.R. §2432.3(b).

[224] 5 U.S.C. §7116.

[225] 5 U.S.C. §7118.

[226] 5 U.S.C. §7116. FLRA, *A Guide to the FLMRP*, pp. 43-48.

[227] 5 U.S.C. §7116(a)(3). FLRA, *A Guide to the FLMRP*, p. 44.

[228] 5 U.S.C. §§7116, 7103(a)(12).

[229] FLRA, *A Guide to the FLMRP*, pp. 18-19, 45-47.

[230] 5 U.S.C. §7116. FLRA, *A Guide to the FLMRP*, pp. 44-46.

[231] 5 U.S.C. §7116(b)(4).

[232] For instance, an employer commits a ULP if it refuses to honor dues allotment authorizations for a representative submitted by employees pursuant to 5 U.S.C. §7115.

[233] FLRA, *A Guide to the FLMRP*, pp.47-48.

[234] 5 U.S.C. §§7104-7105.

[235] 5 U.S.C. §7104(f)(1). Although the Foreign Service falls outside of FSLMRS jurisdiction, the FLRA provides staff support to the Foreign Service Impasse Disputes Panel and the Foreign Service Labor Relations Board. Federal Labor Relations Authority, *Performance and Accountability Report: Fiscal Year 2011* (2011), pp. 3, 5, http://www.flra.gov/webfm_send/542.

[236] 5 U.S.C. §7119(a).

[237] Federal Mediation & Conciliation Service, 2011 Annual Report, 2011, p. 9, http://fmcs.gov/assetsPublic%20Documents/2011_Annual_Report.pdf.

[238] The Panel also assists in resolving agency-union disputes under the Federal Employees Flexible and Compressed Work Schedules Act. 5 U.S.C. §6161(c)(2)(A).

[239] 5 U.S.C. §7119.

[240] Ibid. FLRA, *A Guide to the FLMRP*, pp. 2-3.

[241] 5 U.S.C. §7123. Generally, parties cannot seek judicial review of the Authority's decision not to issue a ULP complaint, because it is not a final order under the statute. See *Rizzitelli v. FLRA*, 212 F.3d 710 (2nd Cir. 2000).

[242] See, e.g., *National Treasury Employees Union v. FLRA*, 732 F.2d 703 (9th Cir. 1984).

[243] Although direct review is unavailable, parties may have an indirect means to gain review of a Panel order. Courts may grant a review if a party does not comply with the Panel's order. Noncompliance is a ULP, which could be subject to the statute's provisions. See, e.g., *Council of Prison Locals v. Brewer*, 735 F.2d 1497 (D.C. 1984).

[244] FLRA, *A Guide to the FLMRP*, pp. 49-51.

[245] 5 C.F.R. §2423.2.

[246] FLRA, *A Guide to the FLMRP*, pp. 49-50.

[247] Ibid., p. 51.

[248] Federal Labor Relations Authority Office of General Counsel, "The Charge," in *Unfair Labor Practice Casehandling Manual* (2010), p. 14, http://www.flra.gov/webfm_send/497.

[249] FLRA, *A Guide to the FLMRP*, p. 22.

[250] Ibid., pp. 22-23.

[251] Ibid., pp. 22-27.

[252] 5 U.S.C. §7121.

[253] 5 U.S.C. §7121(c). FLRA, *A Guide to the FLMRP*, p. 32-33.

[254] The Authority cannot review awards for disputes involving a removal or demotion for unacceptable performance; serious adverse actions, such as a reduction in grade or pay; employment discrimination allegations; or personnel actions prohibited by statute. Awards for these matters can be appealed to U.S. federal courts. FLRA, *A Guide to the FLMRP*, pp. 38-39.

[255] 5 U.S.C. §7122.

[256] Although parties can agree on private arbitration, the agreement must first be approved by FSIP. FLRA, *A Guide to the FLMRP*, p. 28.

[257] 5 U.S.C. §7119(a).

[258] Ibid., pp. 29-30.

INDEX

D

E

F

S

T

U

V

W